PRESCRIPTION FOR A LONG AND HAPPY LIFE

Age-Old Wisdom for the New Age

PRESCRIPTION FOR A LONG AND HAPPY LIFE

Age-Old Wisdom for the New Age

Dov Peretz Elkins

Growth Associates
212 Stuart Road East
Princeton, NJ 08540-1946
(609) 497-7375

Copyright © 1993 Dov Peretz Elkins

ISBN 0-918834-14-7
Library of Congress Catalog Card Number: 93-77902
Printed by Princeton University Press, Princeton, NJ
Printed in the United States of America

All rights reserved.
No portions of this book may be reprinted, copied or photocopied in any form without the express written permission of the author, except for brief excerpts in a book review.

Growth Associates
Human Relations Consultants & Publishers
212 Stuart Road East
Princeton, NJ 08540-1946
(609) 497-7375

To Armin & Adele

With love

and hopes for

a Long and Happy Life

To find no contradiction in the union of old and new; to contemplate the Ancient of Days and all His works with feelings as fresh as if all had then sprang forth at the first creative fiat; characterizes the mind that feels the riddle of the world, and may help to unravel it.

Samuel Taylor Coleridge
Biographia Literaria

Out of the dead letters welled forth songs of life.

Chaim Nachman Bialik

Contents

FOREWORD ix
PREFACE xi

Part I: Age-Old Wisdom for the New Age
PRESCRIPTION FOR A LONG AND HAPPY LIFE 3
AWAKE! 9
MAKE EVERY DAY COUNT 15
THE TZEDAKAH HABIT 21
NINE PRINCIPLES OF ZEDAKAH IN JEWISH THOUGHT 25
JACOB'S LADDER 29
YETZER HA-RA 33
IT'S ALL IN THE ATTITUDE 37
PAUL NEWMAN: THE NEW HOLLYWOOD IMAGE 41
LOVE AS A SONG OF SONGS 45
IDOLATRY 51
THE UNIVERSAL NEED FOR AFFIRMATION 55
LESHON HA-TOV: A GREAT MITZVAH 61
THE CHUTZPAH CONTROVERSY 67

Part II: Judaism for the New Age
SHABBAT AS FANTASY 73
MYTH 83
EMPATHY: MESSAGE OF PESACH 89
ROSH HASHANAH — A SECOND CHANCE 95
THE MITZVAH OF SUKKAH IN THE NEW AGE 101
VE-CHAI BAHEM — TO LIVE BY THEM 105
INGREDIENTS OF A JEWISH CELEBRATION 109
WHY KASHRUT? 113
REFLECTIONS OF AN AMERICAN JEW 117
IS JUDAISM A VINDICTIVE RELIGION? 121
CREDO OF A MODERN JEW 127
REQUIREMENTS OF A CONSERVATIVE JEW 129

Part III: Jewish Concerns and Institutions
THE JEWISH FAMILY 135
WHO NEEDS A SYNAGOGUE ANYWAY? 143
GIVING FORM TO OUR IMAGINATION:
   THE SYNAGOGUE SCHOOL IN THE 21st CENTURY ... 147
MY VIEW OF JEWISH EDUCATION 151
CHAIM SHEL B'RACHA
   In Celebration of a Group Wedding for Former Russian Jews   159

THE JEWISH PEOPLE'S OUTSTRETCHED ARM
  Rescuing Ethiopian Jewry 163
TIME TO SPEAK UP FOR JONATHAN POLLARD 167
WHY SOCIAL JUSTICE IS A THING OF THE FUTURE
  Notes for a Lecture 171

FOREWORD

The sermon has come upon hard times in recent years. Many doubt its effectiveness as a teaching tool. In the age of the sixty-second commercial and the quick sound bite, we have all lost the art of listening for any sustained period of time.

Moreover, the sermon makes heavy demands upon the preacher. It requires careful thought, advance planning, creative imagination and faith in the validity of the entire enterprise.

Small wonder then that the sound of the sermon is rarely being heard in the synagogue today. Many a rabbi has substituted dialoguing with the congregation or teaching a lesson. Obviously these alternatives make much lighter demands of the preacher at a time when so many other demands are clamoring for his/her attention. Rabbi Dov Peretz Elkins has refused to accept the devaluation of the sermon. He believes in its effectiveness, and he marshalls all his impressive skills to illustrate its potential power.

Only one who believes passionately that there is no substitute for the inspirational, emotional and intellectual stimulation that a well-crafted sermon can bring can produce the kind of sermons found in this volume in such marvelous abundance.

Rabbi Elkins chooses his themes carefully, develops his argument persuasively, and provides ample illustrations of the points he makes. His illustrations help to clarify his ideas and to bring the message to the listener with greater clarity.

The author is a trained counsellor whose professional background is reflected in the choice of his subjects. His concerns reflect the cares, dilemmas, hopes, aspirations, and frustrations of his listeners. He knows the fears that dwell in every heart, and he gives them a sympathetic hearing. So many of his sermons contain a therapeutic dimension. They are steeped in Jewish wisdom and conveyed in the contemporary venacular.

Experienced preachers will find a veritable gold mine of ideas worthy of the pulpit and sustaining to their listeners. Rabbis who are just beginning their careers will find in the volume ample proof of the potential effectiveness of a carefully planned and architectured sermon. They will then accept no substitutes.

Rabbi Elkins has rendered a genuine service to preachers of all faiths by sharing with us the harvest of decades of his effective preaching. This volume is eloquent testimony to the undiminished role of the sermon as the most effective vehicle to reach the hearts and minds of the congregants.

RABBI SIDNEY GREENBERG

PREFACE

The busy contemporary rabbi who has countless responsibilities in a modern, demanding congregation, may find the task of creating an inspiring and original sermon on a weekly basis, an impossible chore. Some rabbis, like me, consider preaching among the most significant responsibilities of the rabbinate. As my teacher and friend, Rabbi Sidney Greenberg, says in his Foreward, there is no substitute for the well-crafted sermon if the rabbi wants to both instruct and inspire.

During the three decades of my preaching, I have found great personal satisfaction from trying to take ancient words and ideas and transmute them into a meaningful lesson that has significance for today's worshipper. In a Sephardic book of *musar* (Jewish ethics) called *Pele Yoetz (Wondrous Advisor)*, published in Constantinople, in 1824 by Rabbi Eliezer Papo, the author reminds us that preaching from ancient texts is like "causing the lips of those who sleep to speak" (Song of Songs 7:10). He interprets this biblical verse to mean that when sacred words from the past are quoted, the lips of deceased Torah scholars actually move!

In delivering the sermons and talks included in this volume it was my intention to move the hearts of my listeners, and not necessarily the lips of the deceased scholars whom I quote. But I must acknowledge a significant debt to our rich tradition with its profound and abundant wisdom, that has permitted me to interpret and embellish age-old ideas for the New Age. I consider it a great honor and sacred privilege to quote their words and offer my personal interpretations of them to my congregants and students.

Among the master preachers from whom I learned the art of homiletics in my youth were the late Rabbi Mortimer J. Cohen, of my home congregation, Beth Sholom, in Elkins Park, Pennsylvania, and later, Rabbi David A. Goldstein, of blessed memory, of Har Zion Temple, Penn Valley, Pa., where I first served as assistant rabbi (1966-70). During my college years I would often visit Temple Sinai, in the Oak Lane section of Philadelphia, just to hear Rabbi Sidney Greenberg, one of America's great preachers and creative masters of the art of public speaking. I am deeply honored that Rabbi Greenberg, who, with his beloved wife Hilda, have become dear personal friends to Maxine and me (and who was one of the rabbis who married us), has graciously consented to write the Foreward in the midst of his own demanding and prolific rabbinate.

Besides thanking all the members of my congregations in Norfolk, Cleveland, and now in Princeton, New Jersey, for challenging me to write and deliver these sermons with a seriousness that they deserve, I want to express appreciation to a number of others who helped bring this book to completion.

Audrey Katzman, my devoted and able secretary in Cleveland, typed this entire book during her free time before and after office hours. Audrey also helped considerably in making sentences which were designed to be spoken into thoughts which are of interest to the reader as well. Her considerable editorial skills, and her high level of computer literacy, enabled me to publish this book in record time.

A special relative and friend, Dina Gornish, designed the dust jacket, and provided lots of tender loving care along with her talented art work. My dear friends Albert and Audrey Ratner, of Cleveland, have always believed in me and my teaching, and have supported my efforts in countless ways. My step-sons, Jeremy and Yoni Stadlin, are always available to solve a thorny computer problem at a moment's notice.

My beloved wife, Maxine, is my strongest supporter and most helpful critic in preparing, revising and delivering my sermons. I am afraid she is sometimes biased in evaluating her husband's sermons, but I never fail to take her ideas seriously. It is a great joy to share my rabbinic burdens with her. She makes the difficulties lighter, and the successes greater. I would not be the same kind of rabbi without her steadfast love and devotion.

Princeton, New Jersey
Erev Pesach, 5753

Part I:

Age-Old Wisdom for the New Age

PRESCRIPTION FOR A LONG AND HAPPY LIFE

One evening after enjoying a delicious meal in one of my favorite Chinese restaurants, I opened the fortune cookie and read: "You will live long and enjoy life." Today, we don't have to rely on fortune telling alone, but can tilt the odds in our favor by certain things we do and believe. We all hope, in the words of Dr. Ernst Wynder, president of the American Health Foundation, "to die young as late in life as possible."

In the Torah reading for Rosh Hashanah, we read in the *Akedah* story (Genesis 22, the Binding of Isaac), that Abraham took along with him "two of his servants." The Hasidic interpretation of these two Hebrew words, "*shnai n'arav*" is that Abraham, who was 137 years old at the time, took along the "years of his youth" (the same words in Hebrew). It would have been easy for Abraham to refuse to obey God's command to sacrifice his only son, Isaac, by dint of his old age and infirmity. But Abraham brought along "the years of his youth," his youthful vigor and zeal to obey God's command, and did not excuse himself from the divine behest using age as an excuse.

The 1970 census showed that there were 3000 Americans over the age of 100. In 1980, the number had climbed to 14,000. By the year 2000, it is estimated that there will be over 100,000 centenarians. More importantly, today there are over 2.5 million Americans over 85, the fastest growing segment of the population. By the year 2000 there will be 5 million, and by 2040 about 13 million.

In Jewish tradition, we all hope to live "*bis hundert und zvanzig*" — to 120 (the ideal age which Moses attained). After that it's negotiable. How can we assure ourselves that as the years go by, we will bring the years of our youth into our advanced age, that we will still be vigorous and creative even into our 70's, 80's, and 90's — we should all live so long in good health!

Attitude

The first thing we need to live a long and happy life is a positive attitude.

In her book, *Passages*, Gail Sheehy describes life as a series of adult developmental stages. Our task, she explains, is to recognize and manage these stages. Each new step allows us to let go of the previous one with its satisfactions, and find the freshness and richness of the next stage. With the right attitude, we can let go of each previous stage and move on successfully to the next one.

George Burns put it wisely when he said, "You can't help getting older, but you don't have to get old." Getting older is a physical process, but getting old is a state of mind. We must believe that old age can be an exciting time, and chances are that it will! Our beliefs become a self-fulfilling prophecy. Do you remember Browning's poem, "Rabbi Ben Ezra," in which he wrote:

> Grow old along with me,
> The best is yet to be;
> The last of life
> For which the first was made.

Gerontologists tells us that the image of a vital, active, healthy person past 70 may in fact retard the rate of aging among senior citizens simply by model. When we believe that we can live a long and creative life into our 80's and 90's, we may make it come true. A story tells of an old farmer living in a log cabin on a deserted farm. He became a tourist attraction at age 110. Despite his advanced age, the farmer retained a healthy smile and a positive attitude toward life. Once a tourist asked him "Have you lived here all your life?" "Not yet, not yet," snapped the happy farmer.

At age 90, the late Rabbi David Aronson of Minneapolis addressed a USY (the Youth Movement of Conservative Judaism) convention some years ago. He said that there are two kinds of growing: growing big and growing great. In his words:

> Growing big consists of accumulating things from without — a big car, a big house, a big splash, a big sum of money, a big pile.

> Growing great refers to growth from within — a sensitive mind, a noble character, a concern for the welfare of the community. Growing big is exclusive; growing great is inclusive and sharing. Growing big is competitive, growing great is cooperative. Growing big is good if one also grows correspondingly great.

Today we can point to a host of people thought of as great who are in their 80's and who remain vigorous and creative, such as the gentlemen who retired from the Supreme Court in their 80's in recent years, and Ronald Reagan, who remained President of the U.S. until almost age 80. Some of us are finished living at age 25, and some are not done at 105. With the right attitude, we can live on and on. We realize that life is not dependent on the world we see, but rather on how we see the world.

It's a matter of attitude.

Humor and Play

Besides a healthy positive attitude, we must maintain a sense of playfulness and a good sense of humor, and not cling desperately to life with a deadly seriousness. To paraphrase *Kohelet*, there is a time to be serious and a time to relax and have fun.

The late Norman Cousins taught that humor is great therapy, healing both body and soul and helping our brains produce pain-killing substances known as endorphins. Viktor Frankl, the Viennese psychiatrist who survived Auschwitz, taught the same lesson when he wrote that "Humor is another of the soul's weapons in the fight for self-preservation." (*Man's Search for Meaning* p. 42). We Jews worry too much. You may have heard the classic Jewish telegram: "Start worrying — details to follow." We need to laugh more. We should follow the advice of the Book of Proverbs, "In laughter the pain of the heart is eased" (14:13). Laughter implies a happy philosophy of life. A wise person once said that "He who laughs, lasts."

An Open Mind

The third quality that will help us live a long and happy life is an open mind.

The French philosopher, Emile Chartier, wrote that "Nothing is more dangerous than an idea, especially when it is the only one you have." In a similar vein, the anthropologist Ashley Montague recently described a new disease: psycho-sclerosis. He writes: "Like arteriosclerosis — hardening of the arteries — psychosclerosis is hardening of the mind. Sufferers are unable to see and embrace new ideas. They continue to mistake their prejudices for the laws of nature and the more light you admit to the pupil of their brains, the narrower it grows" (*Psychology Today*, Nov., 1977, p. 39).

The story is told of a group of European rabbis who gathered to talk words of Torah. Each scholar brought a biblical verse with the interpretation of one of his pious ancestors, proudly displaying his important lineage and rabbinic ancestry. One young rabbi wrote an entirely new interpretation, as he had no rabbinic forebears. "My masters," he began, "my father was a baker, not a rabbi. He taught me that only fresh bread was appetizing and that I must avoid the stale. This can also apply to learning." In a certain way his message was the most important, moreso than all the dusty messages of past generations: Don't let yourself get stale!

There are always new worlds to conquer . . . but only if we keep our minds open and unfettered.

Caring for the Body

Jews have always considered care of the body an important prerequisite to fulfillment. It used to be thought that the Greeks cared for their bodies while Jews mastered the intricacies of the intellect. Not so. In Deuteronomy we read: "*Ve-nishmartem m'od le-nafshotaychem,*" which has always been interpreted to mean that we must take good care of our physical health (Deut. 4:15). Maimonides — rabbi, scholar, physician to the Egyptian Sultan — stressed in the 12th century that we must care for our body as we do for our soul.

Consciousness about nutrition and exercise is bringing to millions of people not only a longer life but a new richness for the years before and during old age. Exercise has been called the most effective anti-aging pill ever discovered. Physical activity not only firms up our muscles and keeps down our weight, but according to recent research it increases our self-esteem, relieves anxiety and depression, improves attentiveness, elevates our mood with endorphins, reduces chronic pain, and helps make us feel better about our life and the universe. Cardiologists today, instead of prescribing rest, now recommend vigorous walking in cardiac rehabilitation. The body doesn't wear out, they tell us, it rusts out. Throughout the U.S. you will find senior citizens in classes doing yoga, aerobics, swimming, walking, and many other rigorous physical activities.

As a salty centenarian said on his 100th birthday, "If I'd known I was going to live this long, I'd have taken better care of myself."

Spirituality

Spirituality is the final indispensable ingredient in living a long and happy life. The word "enthusiasm" comes from the Greek "enthousiasmos" (the God within you). Enthusiastic people are aware of a special feeling inside — spirituality — which gives them excitement and inspiration. Dr. Herbert Benson of Harvard Medical School, author of *The Relaxation Response*, speaks of "the faith factor." Having a close tie to a spiritual tradition gives one purpose, direction, a sense of the eternal, and opens up the heart to love and universal harmony.

Our connection to an ageless religion helps us feel ageless. Seeing the sweep of time in Jewish history helps us see our own life in the perspective of many millennia. Our fears diminish and we learn to accept our mortality. *Pirke Avot* teaches us: "Repent one day before your death." How do we know when that will be? The answer is that we must always be ready. Each day must be lived as though it were our last — filled with opportunities to serve, to do *mitzvot*. Never put off meaning in life for tomorrow — but rather find in this day opportunities for joy and hope and fulfillment.

One of the great benefits of a spiritual tradition like Judaism is its lesson about the necessity of giving and sharing lest one become locked inside a personal cage. Pablo Cassals once said, "As long as one can admire and love, then one is young forever." We must share ourselves and our love, before it's too late. We can't wait for the eulogy to tell people we love them and what we appreciate about them. As Rabbi Aronson said, "Grow great, not only big." Grow great through sharing, expanding your heart, letting in lots of love and caring for more people in deeper ways.

A nursery teacher had to step out of class for a few minutes, so she left 4-year-old Ann in charge. When she came back she found 8 little toddlers sitting quietly, watching Ann as she went around the room, saying to each student, one at a time, whispering, "You are precious, you are precious."

These, then, are some important ingredients for a long and happy life: a positive attitude, a sense of play and humor, an open mind, valuing physical exercise and care of the body, and having a spiritual purpose, with a heart full of love. Expect to live long and you likely will. Love yourself and love others. You are precious! Your glowing heart makes you more precious, and gives your heart more energy, life, and joy.

On this New Year, I wish each of you, dear friends — and all Jews and all humanity — a long, healthy and happy life. In the well-known words of the ancient Chinese philosopher, "*Bis hundert und zvanzig!*" Amen!

AWAKE!

Imagine that one morning you had an important appointment — perhaps an interview for a job, or a meeting or a plane to catch on your dream vacation trip around the world . . . and . . . you overslept!

As mortifying as that horrible prospect may sound, such a disappointment pales in comparison with an event on actual record. According to midrashic interpretation, on the morning when God was to reveal the Torah to them on Mount Sinai, the entire people of Israel overslept! For three days they prepared for the great theophany, and when the very special morning arrived, all the thunder and lightning and the blaring voice of the shofar were present in order to awaken the sleeping masses who had almost missed the entire event! (Exodus 19:16, Shir HaShirim Rabba 1:12)

Some authorities maintain that we should stay up all night on *Layl Shavuot* and study (*Tikkun Layl Shavuot*) to compensate for having overslept on the very first Shavuot. In addition, the Jerusalem Talmud informs us that we are not supposed to nap on Rosh Hashanah, the day of the blowing of the shofar, because "He who sleeps during the day of Rosh Hashanah, his *mazal* (fortune), falls asleep too." Other sources tell us that blowing the shofar makes us alert and awake, in more than the physical sense. In the biblical prophet Amos we read: "Shall the shofar be blown in the city and the people not tremble?" (Amos 3:6) In the medieval mystical book, the *Zohar*, the *tekiah* blast is referred to as *Kol Lehitorerut*, a call to be alert and awake.

Perhaps this is where Maimonides, the great 12th century philosopher and law codifier, derived his popular interpretation of the shofar:

> Awake and remember your Creator, you who forget eternal truths by grasping the trifles of the hour. Look well into your deeds and return in repentance. You have lost your way pursuing vain desires. Think of your Creator, and heed the call of your souls. Return to the Lord, and God will have mercy upon you. (*Mishneh Torah, Hilchot Teshuvah*, 3:4)

The Call to Awaken

What is the meaning of this call to awaken?

In many religious traditions, sleep implies a state of spiritual lethargy. In the *midrash* about Mount Sinai, the ancient rabbis were trying to say that the people were emotionally and spiritually unprepared for an event as great as Sinai, when God revealed the Torah to us. After all, it was a slave nation, with no experience of God except for what Moshe had told them. This simple, untutored folk was in no way ready for an experience of direct confrontation with the holy God!

Perhaps the message of the *midrash* is that often, when God speaks to us, or when great spiritual events occur around us, or when life manifests itself in some special sacred way, *we may sleep through it!* Therefore, we need the sound of the shofar to awaken us and bring us to a higher level of readiness. After all, who wants to sleep through a momentous occasion such as the giving of the Torah?

Missing the Peak Experiences of Life

We might say that B'nai Yisrael sleeping through the giving of the Torah is a metaphor for missing the peak experiences of life. "Sleep" is also the word the rabbis use to describe the routine response of the average person, in all his simplicity and banality, to life's sacred opportunities.

Rabbi James Ponet, in a meditation written to introduce the blowing of the shofar, tells us that:

> We resist waking up, [we] yearn for a trance-like numbness, . . . [and we] choose to stumble through our days as if in a dream. For we are inertial beings given to drifting with the tide, heedless of our destination. It takes an outside force to stun us. . . to scare us out of our programmed fears, push us kicking out of the 'four cubits' of dull, daily idolatry where, like sleepers, we have eyes but do not see, ears but do not hear, noses but do not smell, hands but do not feel. . . . God created Jews in order to keep newness in the world; it is the task of the Jew to awaken the dawn." (*Orim: A Jewish Journal at Yale*, Autumn, 1986, pp. 127-128)

William James, Harvard philosopher at the beginning of this century, once wrote:

> Everyone is familiar with the phenomenon of feeling more or less alive on different days. Everyone knows on any given day that there are energies slumbering in him which the incitements of the day do not call forth, but which he might display if these were greater. . . . Compared with what we ought to be, we are only half awake.

Psychiatrist Arthur Deikman writes about "the trance of ordinary life" — the tendency in humans to be preoccupied with imaginings, to confine their attention to extremely narrow segments of reality, thus missing much of what life has to offer (*The Observing Self*, ch. 9, "The Trance of Ordinary Life"). Part of the job of growing up, he writes, is to awaken from this "trance of ordinary life."

Let me share with you an odd bit of American history, the story of U.S. President David Rice Atchison. Never heard of him? When President Polk went out of office and Taylor was to succeed him, inauguration day was on Sunday, March 4. Taylor, a religious man, refused to be inaugurated on his

Sabbath, so the inauguration was changed to Monday, March 5. At Sunday noon, when Polk and his vice-president went out of office, the acting president of the Senate, David Rice Atchison of Missouri, was the only one eligible to become President. Atchison was a bachelor, and had been drinking at inauguration parties all of Saturday night, and fell asleep about 3 a.m. on Sunday, March 4. He left word not to awaken him since he was quite tired. He awoke on Monday afternoon at 1 p.m., thus having slept through his entire term as President of the United States.

A New Age

An interesting comparison is made by Dr. Jean Houston, in her book, *The Possible Human*, who describes what life was like in the Dark Ages before humanity was awakened by the Renaissance in the 13th century:

> Mostly life would be a narrow, brutish fight for subsistence, and your human energies would be exhausted in the attempt to keep your metabolism going. It is the Dark Ages and its shadow falls across your mind and dulls your spirit. (p. xii)

> A rhythm of awakening is needed, and it comes in the form of the Renaissance, with its revival of ancient philosophy and myth, literature, and science. Ideas and images are excavated from their Greek, Roman and Hebraic origins, forgotten texts are translated, esoteric attitudes become available. A veritable archaeology of the Western world's past thoughts and dreams is unearthed, and the horizon of what it means to be human is extended. (p. xiii)

A new consciousness is emerging, a new Renaissance, awakening the slumbering giant of modern technological society from a deep sleep. Moshe received the Torah and brought a new awakening to a people who would rather have slept through life, radically changing their lives by giving it form, purpose, and direction. The Renaissance, the Awakening, shook up a people too long lying in the darkness of ignorance, poverty, squalor, and inequity. So, too, today, we are being awakened by a new generation which is seeking a higher quality of cultural and spiritual life: deeper relationships, better families, more effective education, justice for the poor, the sick and the hungry, more creative pursuits in the work place, and a redefined role for women that permits their real, full self to emerge. As Jean Houston states, "the depths start to rise, and the other side of the moon of ourselves haunts our becoming and demands its tribute. It is the first stirrings of the Rhythm of Awakening" (p. xv). This is a new Renaissance era of personal fulfillment, self-realization, and higher spiritual evolution.

On Rosh Hashanah, the shofar arouses us from the "trance of ordinary life." It comes to prevent us from missing life by sleeping through it, like Rip Van Winkle who saw a picture of King George III when he went to sleep, and after he awoke saw a picture of George Washington. He had slept through a revolution. We dare not sleep through the revolution that is taking place in our own day, before our very eyes!

Too many of us sleep through life, with its many opportunities for growth, learning and development, by being couch potatoes and watching TV. The television is turned on in the average American household for 7 hours a day! By the end of his life, John Doe of Main St., USA will have spent ten years in front of the set. The blaring of the TV day and night makes us into passive zombies, glued to a screen portraying violence, sex, extra-marital affairs and dysfunctional families. It keeps us from getting to know members of our own family, reading a good book, and developing the art of conversation.

Two Mitzvot

Two mitzvot are indispensable to revive and reawaken Judaism in our generation: Kashrut and Shabbat. Let's take them one at a time.

1. Kashrut awakens our religious and ethical consciousness on many levels. As our consciousness expands regarding healthy eating habits, we should expand the meaning of Jewish dietary laws. New prohibitions could include preservatives, additives, artificial coloring, excessive amounts of sugar, salt, fat, or cholesterol — all the things which we stuff into our mouths without thinking, poisoning our bodies, giving ourselves premature cancer or heart disease, and violating one of Judaism's sacred principles of treating our body with honor and respect.

   The message comes to us via many avenues — the medical community, ecology groups, the government, even from our own children — yet we continue to pretend that we don't hear. We remain asleep while our bodies are destroyed. It's time to wake up, and stop putting caffeine, nicotine, and other pollutants into the sacred vessel which houses our soul.

   Further, we need to pay more attention to the whole eating experience, and to elevate it, as Judaism demands, to a sacred act. We should say a prayer of gratitude before and after we eat, eat slowly and carefully, and share the surplus with the hungry instead of tossing it into the garbage. We can recycle our waste products instead of fouling the environment with them.

2. We also sleep through life by ignoring the regenerative power that Shabbat can bring to our lives and to our families.

   There is an old and hallowed tradition that Shabbat afternoon is a wonderful time to catch some extra winks. Nevertheless, the remaining time during Shabbat we could be much more awake to the beauty of the constellation of its traditions: from Friday night candles, kiddush, blessing the children, family singing of *z'mirot* and *Birkat Ha-Mazon*, to attending worship on Shabbat morning, *Seudah Shlishit* and *Havdalah* on Saturday night, and the myriad opportunities for friendship, study, and reflection that Shabbat offers.

If the Jewish people are to truly awaken to the magnificence of our priceless heritage, Shabbat observance must be a more vital part of our weekly routine. We shall have to sing more, be silent more, feel awe more, hope more, praise more and love more. If you observe Shabbat in some meaningful way for just a few months, your entire life will change. And the beauty of that one day a week will begin to penetrate and transform all the other days as well.

Increased Spirituality

Lastly, to be truly awake in this age of renewed consciousness, we need to devote more time and energy to our spiritual selves. Our young people have for too long been disillusioned with the spiritual emptiness of Jewish institutional life, including the synagogue. We must find ways to bring more spiritual depth into our personal lives as well as into our synagogue experience.

We need to become more familiar with the majestic beauty of the *Siddur* and the *Mahzor*, with the poetic phrases and ideas that have the power to awaken us from our spiritual slumber and lethargy, and call forth within us a new appreciation of life's blessings.

So much of the underlying theology of Rosh Hashanah points in the direction of being born again, of awakening on the morning of the New Year to a new life and a new way of life. *Hayom Harat Olam* — this is the birthday of the world. This is the first day of the rest of our lives. It is the time to awaken to the infinite possibilities latent within our souls. The pious Jew finds this invitation in the first sentence of the 16th century Code of Jewish Law, the *Shulchan Arukh*: Arise like a lion in the morning for the service of the Creator!

Hayom Harat Olam! As Thomas Paine stated in his call to arms: "We have it in ourselves to begin the world again." In 18th century France, Count de Saint-Simon instructed his valet to wake him every morning with these words: "Wake up, monsieur, you have great things to do today." The shofar calls to each of us: Wake up! You have great things to do this year!

MAKE EVERY DAY COUNT

I begin with a parable of Rabbi Chayim of Zans.

> A poor country woman had many children who were constantly begging for food and she had nothing to give them to eat. One day she found an egg. Excitedly she called her children, "Children, children, we have nothing to worry about any more. I have found an egg. But being a provident woman, I will not eat the egg, but rather I will ask my neighbor for permission to set it under her hen, until a chicken is hatched.
>
> "We will not eat the chick, for I am a provident woman! Rather we will wait til she grows into a hen, set her on her eggs, and the eggs will hatch into chickens. And the chickens in their turn will hatch many eggs, and we will have many chickens and many eggs.
>
> "But we will not eat the chickens and the eggs, for I am a provident woman! We shall sell them and buy a calf. And we will not sell the cow until it has calves. And we will not eat it then, either, but wait until we have many cows and calves.
>
> "Then I will sell the cows and the calves and buy a field, and we will have a field and cows and calves, and we won't need anything any more!"
>
> The poor country woman was excitedly planning for the future made possible by this wonderful egg, when suddenly it dropped out of her hands and broke.
>
> Said Rabbi Chayim of Zans, "See, my students, this is how we are when the holy days arrive. Every person resolves to do *Teshuva*, repentance, thinking in his heart, 'I will do this and that,' but the days slip by with only deliberation and planning that does not lead to deeds. Before you know it, nothing changes, nothing happens, and the next year merely repeats the previous one."

Rabbi Chayim's parable contains a penetrating message. Sometimes we have the best intentions, and we think, wait, and dream, and somehow, before we are able to take action, it is too late. Our lives go by in the same way, with little change and little of our suffering alleviated, and we fall a little deeper into the same old rut.

On Yom Kippur we recognize most poignantly the relentless march of time, with the realization that we have not lived up to our hopes and dreams. Rabbi Sidney Greenberg notes that:

> The film of life cannot be rewound. . . . Sometimes we come to a moment so exquisite that we understand the poet's plea: "O moment stay, thou art fair." But we cannot stop time in its track. What can we do with time? Many things. We can kill it, we can waste it, we can use it, we can invest it. Prisoners serve time, musicians mark time, idlers pass time, speeding motorists make time, referees call time, historians record time, scorekeepers keep time. . . . Once it is gone, it is irretrievable. Horace Mann once put this announcement in a newspaper's lost-and-found column: "Lost, somewhere

between sunrise and sunset, two golden hours, each set with 60 diamond minutes. No reward is offered, for they are gone forever." Like money, time has a way of slipping through our fingers with nothing to show for it. (*Jewish Exponent*, 9-28-84)

How can we invest our time so that we will not fall into a trap as the poor country woman did in Rabbi Chayim's parable? How can we fulfill the vision of the Psalmist, "Teach us to use all of our days, That we may attain a heart of wisdom" (Psalm 90)? How can we avoid that terrible nightmare that so many of us fear, that we may, in the words of the Siddur, live in emptiness and give birth to futility ("*lemaan lo niga lareek, ve-lo neled labehala*")?

Like the woman in the parable, all of us dream of great things. But if we dream too much and take no action, then the egg is dropped, the dream is aborted, and nothing is achieved. We need to learn to invest our time judiciously so that when our end comes, we will have no regrets. Several examples will illustrate.

Another Day — Another Mitzvah

Henrietta Szold told of an incident which occurred when she visited a poverty-stricken ghetto shortly after World War I. She met a man, bent beneath the weight of over 90 years, who had lived a life of poverty and pain. Ms. Szold asked him, "What do you want more than anything else in the world?" He replied, "Life." Ms. Szold was intrigued by this man, who after nine decades of suffering wanted nothing more than to live longer, rather than find respite and peace from the burden of life. She asked him why, and he replied, "Because every extra day I live can add to the number of *mitzvot* I can perform. Every additional day I have I can add an extra prayer to God, and can do a fellow man a good turn." (Story from Rabbi Chaim Pearl.)

Better Than a Senate Seat

These thoughts of life and death and the proper investment of the precious commodity of time, came to me when reading recently of the life of Paul E. Tsongas, the ambitious Senator from Massachusetts. In his early 40's, Tsongas retired from the Senate after just one term after he was told, in 1983, that he had nodular lymphoma, which could be treated but never cured. His doctors told him he could survive another six-year term, but he chose not to run for re-election. Rather, he opted to live the rest of his life as a "normal" husband to his wife, and father to his three daughters, Molly, Ashley, and Katina. "I was probably the prototypical ambitious person," Tsongas said in an interview, "and that was all very nice, but it ain't no substitute for human relationships."

(The fact that Tsongas later changed his mind, and decided to attempt to run for the presidency, does not invalidate that period in his life, nor his important decision at the time).

How does former Senator Tsongas live his life now? He told an interviewer that he has taken stock of his life, and has discovered that "No one on his deathbed ever said, 'I wish I had spent more time on my business.'" Tsongas tells the story of how one day, while walking with his young daughter, Molly, in Washington, a motorcyclist pulled up and said, "She's better." "Excuse me?" he asked. "She's better than a Senate seat." And with that, the cyclist roared off. Now, instead of spending every weekend dealing with political business each weekend, he relaxes the time with his family.

Tsongas said that he was sorely tempted to run for the Senate again, as he enjoyed the attention and power. "But I would not have helped Ashley on her science project or accompanied Katina on her brownie weekend camping trip or had Molly fall asleep in my arms in the hammock. . . . Life is a search for balance. We all have to bring the scales back to center" (*NY Times*, 3-18-85). Tsongas decided to life his life according to the wise advice of the great jurist Oliver Wendell Holmes, who said, "As life is action and passion, it is required of a man that he should share the passion and action of his time at peril of being judged not to have lived."

Live Deliberately

Holmes' words bring to mind the philosophy of another great American, Henry David Thoreau. Do you remember the great experiment for which Thoreau is famous? He built a log cabin on Walden Pond in Concord, Mass., and lived in the woods from July, 1845 to September, 1847. After two years, he concluded:

> I went to the woods because I wished to live deliberately, to front only the essential facts of life, and see if I could not learn what it had to teach, and not, when I came to die, discover that I had not lived. I did not wish to live what was not life, living is so dear; nor did I wish to practice resignation, unless it was quite necessary. I wanted to live deep and suck out all the marrow of life, to live so sturdily and Spartan-like as to put to rout all that was not life, to cut a broad swath and shave close, to drive life into a corner, and reduce it to its lowest terms.

Thoreau belongs to a small club of individuals who have chosen to live life fully and completely — not to dream of what might be, not to hold back in order to plan for some great future time, and then to be sorry when the egg breaks before it is hatched, but to squeeze every drop out of life now, <u>today</u>.

Do What You Care About

A young educator, Dr. Harold C. Lyon, Jr., told of an airplane ride during which he sat next to an elderly gentleman. Realizing that he had never really had the opportunity to relate to older people, and never having known either of his grandfathers, he decided to ask his seat mate what was the most important lesson of his life. The older man said he had been a hard-working engineer who had retired at age 70. The most important lesson, he said, was that <u>now</u>, at 87, he was able to travel whenever and wherever he pleased, and "to be free to do for and give to other people. The act of giving to another cannot be taken away. It is an immortal act. 'You only get to keep what you give away.'" The old man now made small pieces of furniture for his grandchildren and great-grandchildren, thoroughly enjoying giving of himself to them. Dr. Lyons continues:

> [The old man's story] reminded me of the Neil Diamond song, "Morningside," about the wooden table he found that had inscribed under it "For my children" — obviously made by an old man who had died and whose children, sadly, hadn't claimed or held on to this gift. Yet the act of giving still can't be taken away. The old man got to keep the act of giving.

At this point in his story, Dr. Lyons comes to some significant conclusions about himself and his own life:

> I began to wonder about my life, Would I wait until age eighty or so to really be free to do the things most important for me — the things that really count? Perhaps I wouldn't live that long. Many people die in the rat race that their lives have become without having what the old man had finally found. (*It's Me and I'm Here!* NY: Delacorte Press, 1974, pp. 151-2)

I don't want that to happen to me! I want to do the things I care about now.

Learn to Live Better

Sometimes it is a chance meeting with a stimulating conversationalist, or perhaps it is an illness that brings us closer to the more profound lessons of life. In the case of Rabbi Harold Schulweis of Encino, California, it was the latter. A few years ago, he suffered a major heart attack, and subsequently shared his thoughts about the experience. Not all of his thoughts were heavy and serious; in fact, some of them were quite humorous. Rabbi Schulweis was brooding in his hospital bed, whereupon his nurse suggested that he watch some television so as not to think as much about his problems. Rabbi Schulweis recalls:

> As I watch during the early hours, transfixed at the ordeals of [the soap operas], and see the tormented, twisted creatures truly suffering from rapes and murders, amnesia and suicide, sadism and infidelity, I chastise myself. "By what right do I complain about a major myocardial infarction compared to their anguish?" Thank you, Nurse.

Other reflections of the good rabbi are a bit more serious and very much worth our noting.

> Some say that there are no atheists in intensive care units and none in the

waiting rooms of hospitals. I don't believe that. To be scared into faith is to inherit a sick faith. The fear will not last, nor will the faith. But faith may come out of a crisis because it bends the tin of your iron will. When the debris and the clutter of the armored self clear away you may begin your rediscovery. Old-new questions reappear. What and who is most important in your life? These questions call for self-revelation and for confessional. This moment, this hour, this day is most important. Do you know whether you will have another like this one? Do not neglect the present tense. And this one sitting beside your bed. Will there be another like this one? No book held in my hand but this human hand held in mine makes me strong, helps me struggle against submission.

In the hospital, I remembered what my mother told me when she was in the hospital. Always she spoke to me in English, except this time. In Yiddish she whispered, "You know, if I get well I promise you I will know how to live better." I don't know precisely what she had in mind, but she never had the chance because for her the rediscovery came too late. We need not wait for a calamitous event to open our eyes to this hour and to those who are about us. Recovery is a return. Go home to your families and love them. Go home to your houses with your Sabbath lights and wine and white challah and make peace. Go home to your families and bind the injured relations. Cast aside your invective and sharpness of tongue and irony and sarcasm and judgment and blame. Go home to your family and learn to listen and enjoy and share legend and story and laugh together, sing together and study together and come to shul together. And go home to your friends. Do not let small things, jealousies, demeaning envies destroy the health in your life.

"Blessed art Thou who fashions persons in wisdom and endows them with health."

The lesson of his illness served Rabbi Schulweis very well. As a scholar and teacher, he was able to heed the warning his life's turn had given him and learn from it. Though some of us have already learned this lesson through our own life experiences, all of us need to hear it again, to be reminded once more as the New Year begins, and as we turn to Yizkor to recall the lessons of those who have gone before us.

We can cultivate an attitude toward life that enables us to enjoy our existence by doing mitzvot, helping others, thinking about what we want from life, and by taking advantage of it now. We can spend our precious time with our loved ones, and with the projects in life which give us the most enduring spiritual satisfaction.

Affirm Life

Such an outlook is described by Robert Muller, former Undersecretary General of the United Nations:

> The key . . . is love, affirmation of life, thankfulness for life. Some have called it sanctity of life . . . , reverence for life . . . . celebration of life. . . .
> I prefer to call it passion for life, the key to all, the result of a personal,

determined decision. Whatever its name, anyone who receives the gift of life ought to feel fathomlessly indebted to it, for he has been given a unique treasure in the universe. He is a true miracle on a planet that is itself a miracle. He should love life from deep within, whatever others may think or proclaim, despite the wars, the prisons, the injustices, the struggles, the inequalities, the false values, the dogmas, the noises, the ideologies, the jealousies, the fashions, and the contortions of the [five] billion human fleas jumping around him. I live, therefore I am. Life is all I have. Life is beautiful, divine, miraculous, fathomless. Life is to love, to do, to learn, to think. to imagine, to talk, to receive, to feel, to understand, to mate, to give birth, and to embrace in one's heart and brain the entire creation. Every moment of life is creation. In every human life all can be accomplished. Man can taste totality and eternity. He can penetrate the infinitely small and the infinitely large. There is so much a human can do and experience! The miseries of life are merely specks of dust on a wonderful object of art. Not to revere, not to love, not to wonder, not to be impassioned with the miraculous, brief droplet of life is a crime, a waste, an outrage. (*Most of All They Taught Me Happiness*, Image Books, 1985, p. 206)

These are our teachers on this Yom Kippur: Rabbi Chayim of Zans, Henrietta Szold, Senator Paul Tsongas, Henry David Thoreau, Dr. Harold Lyon, Rabbi Harold Schulweis, and Robert Muller. In a way their message is one message, the message of the Psalmist: Teach us to count our days, to make every day count, that we may attain a heart of wisdom. It is the message of the prophet Isaiah, who spoke of the future of the people of Israel:

> They shall not toil to no purpose;
> They shall not bear children in vain,
> But rather they shall be a people blessed by the Lord.

May God bless us all with a good life, a full life, a rich life, a generous life, a life of mitzvot, a life of purpose and meaning, a life of joy and of love . . . a life in which we bless each other, and each of us is blessed by God.

THE TZEDAKAH HABIT

"The longest road in the world," says an old Yiddish proverb, "is the one that leads from your pocket." While we poke fun at the natural human reluctance to give charity, Jewish history testifies to the fact that generosity among Jews far surpasses that of other ethnic and religious groups. Like all other habits, the charity habit is ingrained in the earliest years, in the Jewish home.

The word *tzedakah* means "righteousness." More than charity, tzedakah is giving out of duty and responsibility, whether the spirit moves us or not. The Jewish hand must always accompany the Jewish heart. The late Rabbi Abraham Joshua Heschel once wrote that the righteous person is not one who does good deeds, but rather one who is in the *habit* of doing good deeds. Through making tzedakah a part of family life, we can foster the *tzedakah habit* at home.

Personalization

Repetition is the key to inculcating an important value. To learn the tzedakah habit, a child must observe and hear about tzedakah frequently. Giving must be a regular subject of conversation in the home. Among the stories told at bedtime, some should include the theme of tzedakah (see Azriel Eisenberg's collection *Tzedakah: A Way of Life*, Behrman House, 1963). Table conversation should include discussion of searching for and giving to worthy causes.

Each family can seek out special places to donate tzedakah. In addition to regular channels, such as Hadassah, Jewish Federation, UJA (United Jewish Appeal), etc., parents and children should be alert to specific individuals and institutions with which they can share their resources. Opportunities for tzedakah might include a newly-arrived Soviet family, a local hunger fund or soup kitchen, a senior citizens' home, or a Hebrew-speaking camp. While an annual contribution to local umbrella agencies (Jewish Federation, United Way) should remain the focus of the family's largest gift, additional avenues should be sought to help the family establish closer *personal* ties with specific causes. The emotional distance between the parents' checkbook and a resettlement agency in Europe is too great to bring home the importance of making tzedakah a regular family habit.

Contributions to personal tzedakah funds should be made on a frequent and regular basis. Identifying causes and programs can be an on-going process, and the opportunities for giving are endless. Personalized tzedakah contributions can be made in honor of others on life cycle simchas (wedding, baby-naming, Bar/Bat Mitzvah), sad occasions (death, yahrzeit), and milestones (birthday, new job, graduation). At these times, tzedakah is a fitting way to honor those whom we care about. Most organizations send a notice to the honoree that a contribution has been made and by whom. With happy and sad occasions occurring with some degree of frequency, each family should have ample opportunity to decide together on the amount of the contribution, the recipient, and other details related to the gift. Making giving an occasion shared by the entire family will insure that the message of making tzedakah a habit will be firmly imprinted on the mind and heart of each family member.

Family Tzedakah Fund

In Jewish tradition, everyone is obligated to give tzedakah. "Even a poor person, the subject of charity, must give tzedakah," advises the Talmud. According to Jewish Law, one should give not less than 10% and not more than 50% of one's income to tzedakah. However, who participates in the family's contributions is a question not considered carefully enough by most families. Usually, Mom or Dad writes a check and the matter is quickly settled. Why not create a Family Tzedakah Fund out of which contributions can be drawn? In that way, each family member can contribute and become personally involved.

Making regular contributions to the Family Tzedakah Fund should be considered a normal and routine process for each member of the family. Children can contribute from allowance or from money earned from small jobs. Some families make giving tzedakah a condition on which allowance is granted. Bar/Bat Mitzvah children can make their special event more meaningful by sharing a portion of their gifts with one or more causes of their choice.

Danny Siegel, in his book on personalized tzedakah, *Gym Shoes and Irises*[1], quotes a wedding invitation which asks guests to make gifts to tzedakah instead of to the bride and groom.

A NOTE TO OUR RELATIVES AND FRIENDS

> The custom of offering gifts to a betrothed couple stems from the time when people married at very young age, while their families and to some extent the community as a whole still had responsibility for their maintenance and support. We feel fortunate to live in a society of tremendous affluence, and in an era when we as adults choose our own marriage partner and lifestyle.
>
> Our household is already overflowing with a sometimes overwhelming number of seldom-used items. We would like to request, therefore, that your good wishes that might otherwise take the form of presents to us be channeled instead to *tzedakah*. Please consider a donation in honor of our wedding to any of the following:
>
> Action for Soviet Jewry, The American Association for Ethiopian Jews, Tay-Sachs Prevention program, Oxfam-America, Ziv Tzedakah Fund, Inc.

---

[1]Town House Press, 28 V Road, Spring Valley, NY 10977 — one of the best resources a family can have for finding specialized institutions for making family gifts

Non-Monetary Giving

Besides giving dollars, it is often meaningful to donate other items, such as clothing, toys, and food. A Hebrew Day School in White Plains established a project through which students would buy an extra item during grocery shopping, and at the end of each month would bring the food collected to school, delivering it together to various social service agencies in the area. In the publicity describing the project, the school quoted from the *midrash*: "Rabbi Tanhum, though he needed only one portion of meat for himself would buy two; one bunch of vegetables, he would buy two — one for the poor and one for himself." By buttressing the act of tzedakah with biblical and talmudic sources, the act takes on the holy and special category of *mitzvah*, which endows it with a divine aura, and places the act of tzedakah in the proper educational and religious context.

Other non-monetary gifts that the family can donate include furniture to newly arrived immigrants, toys to children's homes, and used clothing to groups that aid the poor. When a family travels to Israel, they can take used toys and clothing to give to orphan homes and residential schools for handicapped children. (Addresses of many such institutions are found in *Gym Shoes and Irises*, pp. 23-30.)

During one trip to Israel with my then-teenaged children, I made a point of visiting several people who distribute funds to worthy individuals. One was the famous rebbetzin, Bracha Kapach (12 Lod Street, Jerusalem), who is considered the Mother Theresa of Israel. Another was a group called *Isha Le-Isha* (Woman to Woman), a battered women's shelter in Jerusalem. If your family will not be visiting Israel this year, why not allocate some money from the Family Tzedakah Fund to give to people who will be visiting Israel? Make them your *sh'liach mitzvah* (an agent to do a mitzvah). Visitors to Israel could also bring clothing or toys to distribute in your name.

The Tzedakah Box

One of the best projects I know of for teaching the tzedakah habit at home is the ancient custom of having a special tzedakah box for dropping coins and bills. The tzedakah box has been a fixture in Jewish homes, schools, and synagogues from time immemorial. In preparation for Shabbat or Yom Tov, members of the family customarily empty their pockets into the tzedakah box. Jewish organizations such as the Jewish National Fund have helped people develop the tzedakah habit during the decades prior to Israel's statehood as a way to foster Zionist consciousness. However, the old blue JNF *pushkes* are found less often in today's homes. Reviving this venerable custom today would go a long way in promoting tzedakah consciousness.

On a table in my living room sits very proudly a beautiful burnished royal blue ceramic cylindrical tzedakah box with the Hebrew word *tzedakah* in raised white lettering on its side, executed by Philadelphia artist Maxine Rosen. Its presence graces the decor of my home and it happily announces a cherished value in the Elkins household. It reminds me before Shabbat and holy days to empty my pockets and share my blessings with the needy.

Children and parents, together and separately, can be encouraged to create their own artistic tzedakah boxes. They will be a significant addition to the furnishings of any Jewish home. When the *pushke*, as the tzedakah box has been called in Yiddish, is filled, it can be emptied and counted by the entire family. The contents can be added to the Family Tzedakah Fund, or distributed independently. Family members can be assigned the various tasks in execution of this special project. One person takes the money to the bank and exchanges it for a money order or a bank check. Another can write the letter(s) to the recipient(s) explaining why they were selected by the donors. Receipts and replies, if there are any, can be read at a family meeting or at a family dinner.

In a letter to Danny Siegel, Rabbi Jack Riemer of Miami, Florida, tells this story about his mother's tzedakah boxes:

> I have just come back from sitting shiva for my mother *z'l* [may her memory be a blessing] . . . This shiva had many highs and lows in it, moments of laughter as we remembered funny stories, moments of pain as we realized that a world was no more. . . .
>
> My son came to the funeral. What do you give a son as a *yerusha* (inheritance)? There was a wall full of tzedakah boxes that she would fill each week before candle lighting. I gave him one. We opened it and found a note in my father's handwriting. He had written: I owe this tzedakah box 29 cents. I paid the debt. Isn't that a nice memento?

What a *yerusha* it would be to all of the young and old of this and the next generation if we could perpetuate the idea of personalized tzedakah! For, as the midrash tells us, tzedakah does at least as much for the giver as it does for the receiver — and perhaps more.

Will making personalized tzedakah a habit change the world? *Pirke Avot* (Ethics of the Fathers) thinks yes: He who increases tzedakah increases peace.

NINE PRINCIPLES OF ZEDAKAH IN JEWISH THOUGHT

The Jewish concept of zedakah encompasses nine principles which are reflected in ancient and modern, secular and religious thought.

1. **We don't own anything. God does.**

   We are stewards, guardians, watchers, and tenants, not owners, of all we find here on earth. Therefore, our responsibility is to preserve and protect our natural resources, and not abuse or exploit them.

   The earth is the Lord's and the fullness thereof, the world and all its inhabitants.
   — Psalm 24:1

   "Give Him of His own, for you and whatever is yours are His," says Rabbi Elazar of Bertota.
   — Pirke Avot 3:8

   All you have shall some day be given. Therefore, give now, that the season of giving may be yours and not your inheritors.
   — Kahlil Gibran
   The Prophet

2. **Giving is better than receiving**

   The poor person does more for the rich person than the rich person does for the poor person.
   — Ruth Rabba 5:9

   Zedakah blesses the one who gives even more than one who receives.
   — Midrash, Leviticus Rabba 34:10

   Rabbi Schmelke of Nikolsburg said: "The poor one gives the rich one much more than the rich gives the poor. More than the poor person needs the rich person, the rich is in need of the poor."
   — Maurice Friedman, *A Dialogue With Hasidic Tales*
   NY: Human Sciences Press, 1988) pp. 95-6.

   There is more pleasure in giving than in taking, for all taking is submission and all giving is mastery.
   — Will Durant

   Giving is more joyous than receiving . . . because in the act of giving lies the expression of my aliveness. . . .

   The most widespread misunderstanding is that which assumes that giving is "giving up" something, being deprived of, sacrificing. People whose main orientation is a nonproductive one feel giving as an impoverishment . . . just because it is painful to give, one *should* give; the virtue of giving, to them, lies in the very act of acceptance of sacrifice. . . .

For the productive character giving has an entirely different meaning. Giving is the highest expression of potency. In the very act of giving I experience my strength, my wealth, my power. This experience of heightened vitality and potency fills me with joy. I experience myself as overflowing, spending, alive, hence as joyous. Giving is more joyous than receiving, not because it is a deprivation, but because in the act of giving lies the expression of my aliveness.
— Erich Fromm
The Art of Loving

There is no joy for the self within the self. Joy is found in giving rather than in acquiring; in serving rather than in taking.
— Rabbi Abraham Joshua Heschel
God in Search of Man, p. 399.

3. **Only what you give is really yours.**

Hillel once said to a group of his students: "If a man has 1,000 dinars and gives 300 to the poor, how much does he then possess?" His students answered, "Simple arithmetic indicates that 700 dinars would be left." "Not so," said Hillel. "He truly possesses only the 300 dinars he gave to zedakah. He may lose the other 700 by accident, or in a business venture; or, with luck, he may leave it to his children. Therefore know that all that a person truly possesses for eternity is the money that person gives away."
— Talmud

Not one who has much is rich, but one who gives much. The hoarder, who is anxiously worried about losing something, is, psychologically speaking, the poor impoverished one, regardless of how much one has. Whoever is capable of giving himself is rich.
— Erich Fromm

We make a living by what we get, but we make a life by what we give.
— Winston Churchill

4. **Every Jew is responsible for every other Jew.**

We are a family, and are obligated to one another. Golda Meir referred to the Jewish People as *Mishpacha Achat*.

The power of resistance which has enabled the Jewish people to survive for thousands of years has been based to a large extent on traditions of mutual

helpfulness. In these years of affliction, our readiness to help one another is being put to an especially severe test. May we stand this test as well as did our forebears before us.
— Albert Einstein

If a brother does not help a brother, who will?
— Maimonides

5. **The more you give, the more you have.**

Why does Proverbs 6:23 say, "For the commandment (mitzvah) is a light?" Because just as a light is not diminished when a flame is kindled from it, so he who does a mitzvah [here meaning zedakah] is not thereby diminished in his possessions.
— Midrash

The Almighty has willed that there be two hands in the matter of charity: one that gives and one that receives. Be thankful that yours is the hand that gives. Open a hand of compassion to the poor. Say not, "I will miss what I give." Be like the sheep who give their wool and have no less the next year because they have given.
— Sefer Hasidim

Juliet: "My bounty is as boundless as the sea. . . . The more I give, the more I have to give."
— Shakespeare
Romeo and Juliet

6. **He who brings others to give is greater than the giver himself.**

Gadol ha-m'-aseh yoter min ha-oseh — he who causes others to do [act, give zedakah] is greater than the doer [the giver].
— Baba Batra 9a

7. **Give to your own people before you give to others.**

It is a natural human instinct to care for one's own — one's family and children, before expending energy or resources on others. Expounding on that instinct, is it not also natural for us to take care of our own — the Jewish People — before taking care of others?

If I am not for myself, who will be for me? And if I am for myself alone, what am I?
— Hillel

If there are poor who are your relatives, and poor in your city, the relatives take priority; poor in your city and in another city, the poor of your city take priorities.

— Midrash, *Tanhuma* (*Parashat Mishpatim*, parag. 8)

Elie Wiesel writes, "A lie cannot be the stepping stone to the truth." We interpret his sentiments to mean that denying one's Jewishness to be a "universalist" cannot enable one to be part of society. One can't join society as a universalist, only as a specific kind of human being — a Jew, Christian, Moslem, etc.

8. Zedakah is a barometer of Jewishness.

A story: a man with a bad heart goes to see his physician, who reaches for his hand and takes his pulse. The man complains that it's his heart, not his hand, that's ailing. The doctor answers, "Yes, but when I take your hand and feel your pulse I can tell about your heart." Likewise, the soundness of a Jew's heart can be judged by his/her hand. When the pulse of zedakah does not beat strongly in the life of the Jew, it indicates a weakening of that person's total Jewish commitment.
— Rabbi Israel Moshowitz

We are obligated to be more scrupulous in fulfilling the mitzvah of zedakah than any other mitzvah. If someone is cruel and does not show mercy, there is reason to suspect that he may not be Jewish.
— Maimonides

Amar Rabbi Asi: Sh'kulah zedakah keneged kol hamitzvot. Said Rabbi Asi: Zedakah is equal to all the other mitzvot together.

9. Giving zedakah makes the rest of your wealth and resources legitimate.

Unless one contributes part of his/her wealth for the benefit of the less fortunate, none of it is properly consecrated.

Rabbi Menachem M. Schneerson, the Lubavitcher Rebbe, explains: "The underlying idea was for the first fruits to be a representative portion of the whole harvest; the sanctity of the *Bikkurim* donation was to affect, to permeate and elevate all the fruits remaining, just as a donation of zedakah brings an element of consecration or sanctity into all of one's wealth."

JACOB'S LADDER

One of the most poetic, enigmatic, and mythically rich Biblical scenes is painted in this week's sidrah, describing Jacob's flight when it is discovered that he stole his father Isaac's blessing from his twin brother Esau. Jacob pauses for the night at sunset in a place called Luz (later known as Beth El), not far from where Jerusalem is today. He takes a stone, uses it for a pillow, falls asleep, and dreams. In his dream, Jacob envisions a ladder whose peak reaches into the Heavens, with angels ascending and descending. God addresses the young lad as the God of his grandfather Abraham and his father Isaac, and promises him that he will return and possess the land, and that his descendants will be as numerous as the dust of the earth, and that God will be his personal Protector. That dream has been the source of creative embellishment by artists, poets, musicians, mystics, liturgists, and spinners of mythical tales for 30 centuries.

In *gematria,* the rabbinic science of numerology, the Hebrew word for ladder, *sulam*, equals 130, as does the word for Sinai. Both are places where a human being met God. When Jacob awakens from his dream he is astonished, suddenly grasping that he has been in the presence of God without realizing it! "Surely the Lord is in this place, and I did not know it!" Shaken, he says: "How awesome is this place! This is none other than the House of God, and that [ladder] is the gateway to Heaven." Jacob's ladder is one which every person can climb to reach God's presence, have a vision of speaking with and being with God, and hearing words of protection, promise, and inspiration. The dream shows things to come which are almost too good and too exciting to be true.

Jacob's spirit had been broken in Beersheva, when he decided to flee for his life. Beth El, which had been a desolate spot of earth, was now laden with such potential that it could bridge the gap between heaven and earth. When the shining stairway to the glory of Heaven appears, a sense of extraordinary wonder overcomes Jacob and restores his faith in his future and in the future of his descendants who were to become the people of Jacob, the people of Israel. As Jacob recognizes perhaps for the first time the great reality of the Divine, he becomes the model for anyone who could suddenly become aware that they too stand at the gateway to Heaven, and can feel God beckoning them to higher and nobler pursuits.

The words of a poet reflect this idea:

> Thou hast made the flowers to bloom
> And the stars to shine
> Hid rare gems of richest ore
> In the tunneled mine.
> But chief of all Thy wondrous works
> Supreme of all Thy plan
> Thou has put an upward reach

In the heart of man. (Harry Kemp)

That upward reach is surely one of the most precious parts of the life of the human soul, yet one of the most severely neglected.

Transcendent Lacking in Jewish Life

One thing our young people complain most about regarding religious education is that it does not afford them a glimpse into the transcendent. Then when some cult figure lures them into a spiritual opportunity, they jump for it. It is one of the saddest things to watch when young Jews look to Eastern religions like Zen Buddhism, or to some phoney, mind-stealing religious quackery to search for God, when in their own rich heritage there exists an untapped mine of mystical experience that awaits their adventurous travel.

Not long ago a feature article on the front page of the New York Times described the burgeoning movement of spiritual retreat centers where Christians and unchurched people go to spend a vacation weekend. There they find the opportunity for meditation, reflection, spiritual renewal, with wholesome food and time for yoga or therapeutic massage. But Jews are frustrated in their search for such a spiritual experience within the confines of the Jewish community. There is no such Jewish retreat center comparable to what our Christian friends have all over North America.

Jacob's Dream a Paradigm

Jacob's dream has been the source for many dreamers throughout Jewish history, who longed to confront God and feel the Divine presence the way Jacob did, seeing the Heavenly ladder stretched out before them, binding them to heavenly spheres.

When the prophet Elijah ran away from the wicked Jezebel into the Sinai desert, he too listened for the comforting voice of God. Like Jacob, he fell asleep, and when he awakened, he walked 40 days and 40 nights until he came to the mountain where Moshe and the people of Israel had met God centuries before. As Elijah stood before the mountain of the Lord, the Lord passed by (I Kings 19), and there was a great wind, splitting mountains and shattering rocks by the power of the Lord. But the Lord was not in the wind. After the wind came an earthquake, but the Lord was not in the earthquake. After the earthquake was a fire, but the Lord was not in the fire. After the fire came a still small voice. And Elijah listened, and like Jacob he recognized that the voice he heard inside himself was indeed the voice of God calling out to him to serve his people. Like Jacob, Elijah's life was changed forever by his encounter with God.

The Hasidic masters taught incessantly about the ubiquitousness of God's presence. The Baal Shem Tov taught his disciples: *let atar panui minay* — there is no spot on earth devoid of God's presence. Regarding the story of Moshe at the burning bush, when God tells Moshe to remove his shoes, for the ground on which he is standing is holy, Rabbi Moshe of Kobryn says that this verse brings a lesson: Removing one's shoes means removing habits of seeing things in the usual way, and realizing that anywhere you stand can be a holy place.

Our Lives, Too, Can be Changed

The ladder from heaven to earth is a paradigm that for the bridge that spans the finite and the infinite. When we climb the ladder, as did Jacob and Elijah, we live not only in the moment, but in the eternal. We feel more connected to our universe and to God; we go beyond our small separated self, and become part of a greater whole. In other words, we transcend our own life and become part of all that God created, with the "great chain of life." As Albert Schweitzer described it, we feel "one with all life that comes within one's reach."

The story of Jacob's ladder is a simple story which teaches us that wherever we stand can be a gateway to heaven, and the place where God lives. God is there to speak to us, reach out and uplift us, and promise us a new role in serving our people and the world. When we feel God's presence deeply, we come away from the experience with broader vision, renewed energy, grander insight, enlarged perspective, and a steadier view of life.

Let me share a personal experience with you.

When I was about 6 years old, my parents sent me to summer camp. I was probably too young to be shipped off to camp all by myself, but it was in the middle of the Second World War, and my mother had to help my father in his business. She just couldn't deal with a more-than-full-time job as well as a 6-year-old, so off I went. One morning I woke up a few minutes before anyone else in the cabin, and I stepped outside and looked at the view. I saw beautiful mountains, and a breathtakingly blue sky, and a blinding red sun rising over the mountain in the distance. It was extremely quiet because it was very early in the morning and the camp had not yet awakened. I just stood there and stared at the ineffable scene.

As young as I was, I knew that there was something very special about what I was feeling and seeing. I couldn't put it into words, but I knew that I would remember that moment for the rest of my life. I had not yet read the story of Jacob's dream or Elijah's still small voice, but when I did read those stories I remembered my short visit with God at Camp Skymount in the Pocono mountains. Once one has such a vision, such a transcendent experience, there is a calm that comes over our lives. We have more patience with people, a greater understanding of what life is really about, less tolerance for pettiness and foolishness, more dedication to the higher things in our world, and a new and profound grasp on the ultimate issues of life. Our being has changed because of our personal vision of God, and nothing will ever be the same after that.

I knew then, when I had that experience as a young child in summer camp, that I might meet God again later in life at other critical junctures — as when I flew over the Swiss Alps in 1962 and looked down from the airplane and saw beautiful snow-capped mountains that sparkled so brightly that my eyes and my soul were blinded when I tried to look directly at them. It was a scene captivating in its beauty. It reminded me of an Ansel Adams black-and-white photograph, except that this scene was in living color and it was real, right in front of my own eyes. The awesomeness of the scene cannot be described adequately in words.

When I watched the birth of my son Jonathan (when Hillel, my eldest was born, the doctor did not permit fathers into the delivery room) and I saw his little head pushing through into the world, I knew that a miracle of such indescribable dimensions was taking place, that it simply had to be that God was in this place. I was so filled with awe that my heart pounded and my soul was irrevocably lifted to a new plane. *Ma nora hamakom hazeh, ayn ze kee im bet Elohim* (How filled with awe is such a place. It can be none other than the very dwelling-place of God).

What happened to Jacob can happen to anybody, any time, any place. God can appear anywhere if we permit the Divine into our heart. We could be sitting in a classroom listening to a young child surprise us with a splendid reply to a simple question. We could be standing in a courtroom, waiting for an act of ultimate justice to be rendered for someone who waited a long time to be vindicated; or we could be sitting at the family dinner table, and suddenly look into the faces of our loved ones and know that God has blessed us, and has spoken to us with special Divine gifts.

All we need to do is want to have a dream as Jacob did, awaken from a deep sleep, and realize that God may have been speaking to us, and we appreciate our blessings in a new way. God is there, and we hear the Voice. We have a new vision of what our life can be, what our destiny is, and where we are to go from here.

From then on, things will never again be the same.

YETZER HA-RA

Two Hebrew phrases, *yetzer ha-ra* and *yetzer ha-tov*, embody our dual inclinations to good and evil. All of us have both. Our life's task is to let the tendency to good rule the tendency to evil. However, attaining this goal is not so easy.

The story of Samson, Judge of Israel for 20 years, exemplifies the good-evil struggle (see Judges 13-16). Samson, a hero warrior, protected the people of Israel with great supernatural might. He slaughtered 1000 Philistines with the jawbone of an ass (Judges 15:16), killed a young lion with his bare hands, slaughtered 30 men from Ashkeklon and took their clothes to pay a wager, and caught 300 foxes and set them on fire. At the end of his life, he pulled down the temple of the pagan god Dagon, killing 3000 people.

One of the most unusual things about Samson is that he was a Nazirite, one of God's special heroes who takes exceptional vows: not to drink any product of the vine, no razor to touch his head. Samson's story shows a negative religious hero — "an example of what God's charismatic individual should not be." (Interpreter's Dictionary of the Bible, s.v. "Samson"). His tragic story portrays a man ruled by selfish and uncontrolled passion and forgetful of sacred vows, which brings him to disaster. Samson epitomizes the person who has lost control of himself and succumbed to his *yetzer ha-ra*.

Talmudic Discussions

An interesting passage in the Talmud says that when one concluded the period of Naziriteship, he had to bring a sin offering. Why? Because renouncing permitted pleasures is a sin! In other words, drinking wine and exercising libidinal desires are blessings from God. While one must learn to contain them, one retains ambivalence about them. Similarly, we are ambivalent about Samson. He was heroic, but weak; a savior of people, a *Shofet* (Judge), but disloyal, selfish, and self-indulgent.

Pirke Avot defines strength in these words: "Who is really the strong person? One who controls the *yetzer*, one's passion" (Avot 4:1). Samson did not control his passions, and thus was not really strong. Strength lies not in murdering 1000 Philistine warriors, but in mastering one's inner tendencies to power, lust and greed.

The Talmudic rabbis extolled spiritual strength over physical strength, but they were not unaware of the difficulty of overcoming our passions. Their insightful analysis appears in reference to the first chapter of Genesis, the Creation story, in which each day concludes with the phrase, "*Vayar Elohim kee tov*" — "God saw that it was good." At the very end of the story, we read, "And God saw what He created, and behold it was *very* good." The word *very*, used for the first time, shows that what God created was exceptionally good.

Whereupon the Talmud states: "'Very good' refers to the *yezter ha-ra* — the evil inclination. But is the evil inclination **very good**? Yes, for if not for the *yetzer ha-ra*, one would not build a house, nor find a spouse, nor have children" (Midrash, Genesis Raba 9:7). In a related passage, the rabbis comment on the words in the Sh'ma: "You shall love the Lord your God with all your heart" (Deut 6:5). The Rabbis take word *le-vav'cha*, spelled with a double *bet*, and note that the word for heart, *lev*, has only one *bet*. They explain that one must love God with a double *yetzer* — both the **good** and the **evil** *yetzer*.

Definition of Yetzer

What is *yetzer ha-ra*? Not really evil, it is more akin to neutral. If you let it alone, without control, it can become evil. It is really your passions, which can be a most positive force.

In fact, the rabbis also said that *Gadol ha-adam, gadol ha-yetzer* (the greater the man, the greater his *yetzer!* — Talmud, Sukkah 51b). In other words, don't think that great people are the ones who have subdued their *yetzer ha-ra*; to the contrary — the greater people are the ones who have not killed their *yetzer*, but who keep it in check, and use it for a positive purpose.

One rabbi taught that people can be divided into three categories: the saint, in whom the *yetzer ha-tov* rules; the wicked, in whom *yetzer ha-ra* rules; and the rest of us, most of the world, in whom both rule (Talmud, Berakhot 61b). Thus, most normal people require both! One really can not serve God with only one; instead, one serves God with both the *yetzer ha-tov* and the *yetzer ha-ra*!

A Hasidic story tells us that the disciples of the Baal Shem, the founder of Hasidism, ask him how can they know if a certain famous scholar was a true *zaddik* (righteous person)? The Besht (Baal Shem Tov) answered, "Ask him to advise you what to do to keep unholy thoughts from disturbing you in your prayers and studies. If he gives you advice, then you will know that he belongs to those who are of no account. For this is the service of men in the world to the very hour of their death: to struggle time after time with the extraneous, and time after time to uplift and fit it into the nature of the Divine Name" (Buber, *Tales of the Hasidism, Early Masters,* p. 66). In other words, don't listen to anyone who claims to have an easy answer to push out the *yetzer ha-ra*. The struggle remains a daily part of life.

The *yetzer ha-ra* is a ubiquitous companion, and there is no denying it.

In another Hasidic tale, Reb Mendel of Kotzk states, "For having seduced Eve, the serpent was sentenced to forever crawl in, and eat, dust. What kind of punishment is that? asked the Master of Kotzk. Condemned to eat dust, the serpent would never be hungry — is that a punishment? Yes, answered the Kotzker (rebbe). That is the worst punishment of all: never to be hungry, never to seek, never to desire anything" (Elie Wiesel, *Somewhere a Master*, p. 101).

To summarize, the *yetzer ha-ra* is not really evil, only the potential for evil. Our job is to control it with the hard work of living an ethical life, studying Torah, constantly sharpening our values, doing good deeds, and thus not giving the *yetzer ha-ra* too much power in the wrong direction. Steer it — direct it on the right path, but you can not totally eliminate it, because without it you can not live.

Maybe one reason it's called the *yetzer ha-ra* — the evil inclination — is because in so many other cultures and religions, the bodily passions — eating, sex, play — are evil; whereas in Judaism they are not evil, but can be used to serve God. These passions can become evil, if we let them, but we don't have to let them!

Another Explanation

One final explanation of the *yetzer ha-ra* comes from the great Swiss psychoanalyst, Carl Jung, who wrote of the side of our personality which we don't like to see — our shadow, the parts that we reject or repress. The problem with these elements of ourselves, says Jung, is that if we become unaware that they are part of us, they find a way to emerge, even against our will. For example, if we claim that we never get angry, because we have been taught that anger is a bad thing, then we always smile and act as if we are not angry. However, the anger remains (whether consciously or not, everyone experiences it). It goes underground, builds up steam, and then at some time we may explode.

Consider people who assassinate famous heroes, or shoot up a crowd in a post office or fast food franchise. Their neighbors always describe them as quiet, sweet, harmless people. A televangelist may never admit to himself that he is a normal sexual being, and screams at his audiences that sex is sinful, and if you lust even in your heart, you are evil. Then one day you hear that this person raped his secretary, or one of his parishioners. These types of people deny their shadow . . . and suddenly it bursts forth and controls them.

The *yetzer ha-ra* is evil when we don't admit that it's there, when we deny to ourselves that it's a part of us. If we deny our anger, it leaks out as a passive-aggressive act of covert hostility, or as explosive rage or violence. And if we deny our sexuality, we can preach beautiful sermons about how evil it is, and then one day find ourselves knocked over the head by the hatchet of our own *yetzer ha-ra*.

Examples of such split personalities abound in literature (*e.g.* Dr. Jekyll and Mr. Hyde) where people live two lives — one public, and another repressed and denied so long and so strong, that it comes out full blown when least suspected. This shadow part of our personality is the part of ourselves that we wish weren't there. But unless we accept the shadow and turn it into something useful and constructive, we aren't living up to our full potential. By excluding parts of ourselves, we let them grow dark and evil; then they control us instead of our controlling them.

Accept the Yetzer

Thus the *yetzer ha-ra* holds such an important place in rabbinic literature. Without it no one would build a house, marry, or go to work. *Yetzer ha-ra* is our libidinal energy that can be used for positive, wholesome achievements, if only we don't reject it, but direct it, and let it work <u>for</u> us instead of <u>against</u> us.

The potency of the *yetzer ha-ra* lies in its ability to hide and to be denied. Yet when we face it, it works in our favor, not to our detriment. When repressed, *yetzer ha-ra* can be a potent poison, and when faced it can be the yeast in our soul, and help us create a magnificent portrait with our artistic talents. The *yetzer ha-ra* can be our most useful friend, if we know what it is and where it can be found.

In the Jewish community, we deny the existence of alcoholics, juvenile delinquents, child- or wife-abusers, and mental illness. We pretend, close our eyes, and brag about our purity and how superior we are to other ethnic groups. Yet these problems fester because we don't create programs to address them, or assign people to treat them, or teach our children to prevent them. The shadow of our soul becomes our dark brother and eats away at the vitals of our body politic.

How incredibly savvy our rabbinic ancestors were when they saw that a character like Samson was the anti-hero, the weakling who simply let his passions have free reign. Remember the words from the *Pirke Avot*: "Who is truly strong? The one who exercises control over his passions." Also recall that without passion, we cannot possibly serve God. God's most loyal and devoted servants, are the ones with the greatest *yetzer ha-ra*. *Gadol ha-adam, gadol ha-yetzer*. The greater the person, the greater the *yezter*.

When we accept our *yezter*, cultivate and direct it, there is no greater tool or asset with which to serve God. The most passionate servants of humanity are the complete souls who use every fibre of their being to serve God and Divine causes, and to bring healing and redemption to God's ailing and unredeemed world. By loving and serving God with both our good *yetzer* and our bad *yetzer*, we can truly love the Lord our God, with all our heart, with all our soul, and with all our might.

IT'S ALL IN THE ATTITUDE

The first words of today's Sidrah are, "*Vayera aylav Hashem* - The Lord appeared unto Abraham." The phrase seems to be out of context. The ancient rabbis connect it with the last chapter — Abraham's brit milah. From this they deduce the importance of visiting the sick — even God visited Abraham, because he was recuperating from surgery.

Why does God model the mitzvah of *bikkur cholim*? Because it is one of the most important of all the mitzvot. It is included in the Mishna passage in the beginning of the Siddur, "These are the things for which one reaps fruits in both this world and the next: *Bikkur Cholim*. . . ."

Rabbi Akiva elaborates, "Whoever visits the sick removes one part in 60 of the illness of the person visited."

What are the rabbis talking about? Two things: how we are cured from illness and how we heal ourselves from life's inevitable slings and arrows.

Their old/new answer is the human factor — the love factor. Healing has to do with relationships, with *attitude*. Simply put, when people care about us, when we feel loved, we feel healed. Love heals. God healed Abraham just by visiting him, and making him feel loved. Science has a fancy name for it, the new field of psycho-neuro-immunology. In simple language, psycho-neuro-immunology means that the head talks to the nervous system, which tells the body to stay healthy. Abraham and Akiva did not give this concept a name, but they intuited the same thing: how we feel inside our heart changes our physical world (health).

Examples

In Sefer Bemidbar (the Book of Numbers) we find B'nai Yisrael marching in the wilderness and encountering dangerous creatures such as fiery serpents (*ha-n'chasim ha-s'raphim*, Num. 21:6). Many people died, and Moshe had to act. God tells Moshe to make a fiery serpent, a seraph, out of brass, and put it on a pole. Whoever was bitten by a poisonous serpent just had to look at this brass image and would be healed (*ve-ra-ah oto ve-chai*, Num. 21:8).

The Talmud asks (Rosh Hashsanah 29a), "Did the brass serpent really keep someone alive, truly heal a person, just because they looked at it? No, the verse means this: when the Israelites would look up, turn their thoughts on high and subject their hearts to God, they were healed." In other words, it was not magic that healed one, it was God working through the immune system. Looking up, having faith in God, and trusting that God would heal, enabled the sick to become healed.

Let me cite another Biblical verse, this time from Sh'mot (Exodus 6:6). God promises to bring B'nai Yisrael out of Egypt, and tells them, "I will bring you out from under the 'burdens of Egypt,' *Sivlot Mitzraim.*" Why not just say, I will bring you out from Egypt? Why from the "burdens" of Egypt?

The Hasidic master, Reb Simcha Bunam, explains: "The real problem with Jews being in Egypt was not that they were slaves, but that they learned to *accept* it. God saw the Israelites building pyramids, and becoming accustomed to it, and it didn't phase them. God saw that, became upset, and told Moshe, "We have to get them out of here, otherwise they will be slaves the rest of their lives." Their redemption began when they ceased tolerating their slavery. Thus, the Torah says, "God brought you out from under the *burdens* of the Egyptians" (Ex. 6:7). In other words, it wasn't just the slavery, it was the Israelites' *attitude* towards it. In a sense, they were healed, psychologically, morally, politically, when they felt faith in God's redemptive power, when they became fed up with their condition and believed they could become free.

Here again, the *attitude* of the slave, the patient, any of us, is the key to healing, to redemption (cf. Heschel, *A Passion for Truth*, p. 272). In a recent *US AIR* magazine there was a cartoon with the caption, "Attitude brings altitude!"

An Interesting Study

A scientist using computerized California death certificates for the years 1966-1984 found that 25% more Jewish men died the week *after* Pesach than the week before. (I don't think this was related to the heavy matzah balls in the chicken soup!) The researcher, David Phillips of the University of California, San Diego, argued in his paper that men decided to live through the holiday, in order to celebrate with their families. Then he gives examples of the same phenomena in history: both John Adams and Thomas Jefferson died on the 50th anniversary of the signing of the Declaration of Independence. As recorded by his doctor, Jefferson's last words were, "Is it the fourth?" Phillips makes the point that the will to live is a very potent factor. Here again, what our mind tells our body is a powerful message.

The mind can tell the body to get sick, and can also tell it to become well. One's mind can say, "I want to live" or "I want to die"; "I want to be happy and healthy" or "I want to be depressed, miserable, and sick." The only difference lies in our faith, the love we give and get, the courage we exemplify, and the purpose we have to live for.

In an impressive study, two Israeli researchers performed psychological testing on 10,000 men with risk factors for angina pectoris, trying to determine what factors would predict which men would actually develop chest pains. The most accurate predictor turned out to be a "no" to the following question: "Does your wife show you her love?"

Sources and Examples

The Book of Proverbs (16:32): *Tov erekh apayim mee-gibor, U-moshel berucho mee-loked eer.* Better is one who can control his temper than the strongest Rambo; or one who rules over her attitude, her spirit, than a conqueror of a city.

Faith moves mountains! It changes bodies! It heals, saves, and redeems!

Dr. Bernie Siegel, of Yale Medical School, whose books helped make this new field of psycho-neuro-immunology famous, says, "I feel that all disease is ultimately related to a lack of love. . . . I also feel that all healing is related to the ability to give and accept unconditional love." It's as simple as that!

All this may sound pollyannish and romantic, but the scientific evidence is becoming too overwhelmingly large to refute. If we are skeptics and don't believe in the power of faith and love to change *everything*, then we are simply not realists.

The prophet Samuel reminds us of this important lesson (I Sam. 16:7): *Ha-adam yireh la'aynayim — ve-HaShem yireh la-layvav.* We humans see the superficialities of life, but God sees inside. We mortals judge by blood serum, white blood cells, electrocardiograms, and this or that test, but God judges by what's inside the heart. We of flesh and blood see illness, war, oppression, and hatred, and we become victims of the world we see. But God knows — *HaShem yireh la-aynayim* — that we are victims of the way we see the world. For life is 10% what you make it, and 90% how you take it.

God gives us our faces, but we create our own expressions. Or, as John Milton put it, "The mind is its own place, and in itself can make a heaven of hell, and a hell of heaven."

Robert Fulghum, the Unitarian minister who became famous for his folk wisdom, summed it up this way:
> I believe that imagination is stronger than knowledge.
> That myth is more potent than history.
> That dreams are more powerful than facts.
> That hope always triumphs over experience.
> That laughter is the only cure for grief.
> And I believe that love is stronger than death.

(Dedicated to Ron Moses and Shira Kosoy, on their Aufruf, Nov. 14, 1992).

PAUL NEWMAN: THE NEW HOLLYWOOD IMAGE

I was intrigued by the title of a *New York Times Magazine* cover article this week (9-28-86): "Paul Newman: Testing Himself." This is what the High Holidays are all about: testing oneself.

Like some of you, I am a movie buff, and am intrigued by the "heroes" of Hollywood. In the article, Paul Newman is described as "one of the last great movie stars — a legend built up by the old Hollywood studio system at Warner Brothers and MGM and sustained by his magnetism and talent." Newman has acted in 47 films and directed five. He has received an Oscar for "personal integrity and dedication to his craft."

Maybe a person with integrity (how few there seem to be today) merits closer examination. Besides his pretty blue eyes, fame, wealth, power, style . . . is there more to him than the Hollywood sex symbol superstar? So, I read the article, and gleaned some very important things to remind ourselves for the New Year — some lessons about life.

Love and Marriage

I am naturally intrigued by the subject of marriage, especially when reading that Paul Newman is now in his second marriage which has lasted for 28 years! Together, he and Joan Woodward brought three children to their marriage, and they have three of their own. And yes, he says, "I'm still crazy about my wife." It is worth paying attention to long-lasting marriages, especially in Hollywood. Newman discusses the hard work the two of them have put into their relationship, the struggle, the rough spots. Yet, it's worth it, and the marriage works beautifully. It's good to remember the importance of a good marriage.

My thoughts go to the story of Viktor Frankl, Viennese psychiatrist, who was in a concentration camp during World War II. He and a companion were marching out to lay railroad ties in the frozen ground, with guards shouting and driving them with the butts of their rifles. Frankl remembers:

> That brought thoughts of my own wife to mind. And as we stumbled on for miles, slipping on icy spots, supporting each other time and again, dragging one another up and onward, nothing was said, but we both knew; each of us was thinking of his wife. Occasionally I looked at the sky, where the stars were fading and the pink light of the morning was beginning to spread behind a dark bank of clouds. But my mind clung to my wife's image, imagining it with an uncanny acuteness. I heard her answering me, saw her smile, her frank and encouraging look.
>
> A thought transfixed me: for the first time in my life I was the truth as it is set into song by so many poets, proclaimed as the final wisdom by so many thinkers. The truth — that love is the ultimate and the highest goal to which

can aspire. Then I grasped the meaning of the greatest secret that human poetry and human thought and belief have to impart: the salvation of man is through love and in love.

The Importance of Hard Work

When you think of Paul Newman, you think of success, Hollywood, glamour, wealth, a sex symbol, good looks. However, the truth is that Newman was a scrawny little kid. When he began to act, he was denied the parts he wanted. Yes, Paul Newman! So, he began to work out in a gym six hours a day and study acting. He still got terrible reviews. He calls himself a "terrier" — someone who works long and hard to achieve a certain level of performance.

I remember an experience I had as a college student, listening to Maurice Samuel speak on a new book, *The Professor and the Fossil*, dealing with Arnold Toynbee's 8 volume history of human civilization. Toynbee was recognized for his great intellect the world over, yet he called the Jews a Syraic fossil, a dead people. Samuel wrote a refutation, then said something I will always remember: He had to read Toynbee's history five times, to be sure not to charge him with something he did not say. He warned those entering the field of scholarship that it is long, hard work; blood, sweat, and tears. So it is with Paul Newman, and any worthwhile project.

Testing Oneself

The article in the *Times* mentioned that Newman hates complacency. "You have to keep things off balance, or it's all over." He looks for risky roles. For the same reason, he races cars and has won many awards, including the National Championship Sports Car Club of America last year. At age 61, most racers are retired. Yet last month, Newman won an $11,000 first prize purse at the Bendix Trans Am race in Lime Rock, CT. For another challenge, Newman started "Newman's Own," a food company which makes salad dressing, popcorn, and spaghetti sauce, and donates the profits to charity. He really can't stand still!

In a way, this is what Rosh Hashanah is all about: don't stand still. Find a new challenge, be the biggest and best person you can be. Stretch yourself beyond your limits, and when you find that those new limits are comfortable, stretch some more.

Which of these two epitaphs would you prefer on your tombstone:

A. She couldn't try,
    For fear she'd die;
    She never tried,
    And so she died.

B. She couldn't try,
    For fear she'd die;
    But when she tried,
    Her fears — they died.

Compassion

We don't know what kind of Jewish upbringing Paul Newman had, or how he relates to his Jewishness today. The *Times* article says nothing on this subject. But I would like to believe that his sense of compassion, his commitment to social justice and *tzedakah* are related to his being Jewish.

It is well-known that his food business is very successful. This year it grossed $26 million. Since 1982, when he started the company, he has given all of the profits to charity — about $9 million dollars. Some of the charities which have received profits from "Newman's Own" include The American Foundation for AIDS Research, the Cystic Fibrosis Foundation, the Yul Brynner Cancer Fund for Children, and the Kidney Foundation of Canada. All of this from 37 million bottles of salad dressing, 17 million jars of spaghetti sauce, 4 million containers of popcorn, and 1.5 million boxes of microwave popcorn.

Newman's latest project is on a 300 acre forest in northeast Connecticut, with a 47-acre lake, where he is building a summer camp for children with leukemia and other forms of cancer. The camp is staffed with nurses from the Yale-New Haven hospital, and includes facilities for children to receive regular chemotherapy treatments. The camp will offer about 200 children the opportunity to enjoy the outdoors, some of whom only are outdoors when they take trips to and from home and the hospital. Newman and his partner, author A.E. Hotchner, describe the camp as a place where children who would stand out elsewhere would be made to feel comfortable and accepted.

At the news conference announcing the founding of the camp, Newman said, "We felt we had to share the good fortune with others. Besides, there is something repugnant about putting my face on the label and money in my pocket." That phrase I love: "we had to share the good fortune." How many of us have good fortunes? We don't have to be millionaires to have food fortune: health, family, knowledge, and resources. Do we share it? Do we feel that commitment to share it? To give is one of the great mitzvot of Judaism, and one of the greatest satisfactions of life.

The Burden of Fame?

One of the charities to which Paul Newman gives is the Scott Newman Center at the University of Southern California in Pasadena. This is a drug education foundation, headed by Newman's daughter, Susan, named after Newman's only son, Scott, who died at in 1978 at age 28 from an accidental drug and alcohol overdose. I suppose we each have our burdens to bear. Newman bears his bravely, and leads a remarkable and exemplary life.

Here I think of an old Yiddish story. If every human being were allowed to take their pekel of tsuris (bundle of troubles), and hang it on a tree, and then could pick any bundle on the tree, the smart person would pick his/her own! So often we envy others, but when we look behind the veneer, we see that they are not without their own troubles. The smart person is content with his own lot, and is not envious. Rather, as Pirke Avot warns: Who is truly rich, one who is content with his lot.

We think we wish to be Paul Newman. But would it be worth losing a son, to gain the fame, the wealth, and all the rest? Of course not. I'm sure Paul Newman would give it all up if only he could have his son back again. Our lesson: don't be envious. We must accept our lot in life, and work to improve ourselves while not envying others. We must rejoice in what we have.

Rosh Hashanah Lessons

These, my friends, are some important lessons we reflect upon at the beginning of the new year:

1. Work harder at making our marriages and family life successful.
2. Persistence and hard work will bring us rich rewards.
3. Stretch yourself, risk a bit, and find new limits for your capacities.
4. Compassion and *tzedakah* are still the tried and true marks of a good Jew.
5. Contentment arises from satisfaction with our lot, without envy and jealousy of others.

Important lessons, these. Let's take them to heart, and lead a better life.

LOVE AS A SONG OF SONGS

Like old bears lumbering out of winter caves, we stand at the edge of Spring, roused by an unerringly familiar sound, the sound of the earth in transit, the ground of our being on the move. We hear the song of the soul. In India, the sound of Krishna's flute is the magical cause of the birth of the world, and everywhere singing represents the natural connection between all things, and the communication of that link. Out of our own sacred cannon comes the Song (of Songs) whose imagery is a universal expression of the journey of soul-making. Its major theme is that of separation and reconciliation, redressing the split between exile and home, sexuality and spirituality. It is a song of lament and expectation, a love song for the morning of the year.

> In the long winter nights of waiting, we have wandered around in our own interior forest, separate from the world, [as Shir HaShirim puts it:] like "a garden locked, a fountain sealed, charged not to stir up nor awaken love until it please." Yet hibernation that lasts too far into spring often kills what is in bud. Out of the great silence of our cold feet, cold storage, cold war, the ice begins to crack. The earth is at prayer." (Cynthia Hirni, *The Ridgeleaf*, March, 1985, #154)

Pesach and the Song of Songs

On Pesach, we read the biblical book of love poetry, The Song of Songs, attributed to King Solomon — *Shir Hashirim, asher le-Shlomo*. Why do we read Shir HaShirim at this time? First, Pesach is a time for family, the source of and outlet for love. Also, Spring — the time of Pesach — is the time of love. Feel the spring air, the air of love, in its pages:

> My beloved spoke to me: "Arise, my darling; my fair one, come away! For now the winter is past, the rains are over and gone. The blossoms have appeared in the land, the time of pruning has come; the song of the turtle-dove is heard in our land. The green figs form on the fig tree, the vines in blossom give off fragrance. Arise, my darling, my fair one, come away!"

We are lucky that we still have the Song of Songs. Many do not realize that it was almost lost. During the second century, a fierce debate took place among scholars at Yavneh, where canonization took place. The rabbis maintained that Shir HaShirim is an earthly book of physical love. A modern censorship board might say that it lacks redeeming theological value. Truly, in the narrowest sense, this is a secular book: the name of God never appears.

Rabbi Akiva made the difference. A giant of spirit, Akiva saw in human love a powerful divine force: love was all. *"Ze k'lal gadol baTorah: ve'ahavta le-rayacha kamocha!"* He saw the book as a metaphor for the love between God and Israel. Akiva's life was replete with human love: deep romantic love with his wife, Rachel, and the love of God, which he fulfilled when he died as a martyr. When the Romans forbade the study of Torah and practice of Judaism, Akiva became a martyr, and rejoiced in death. He told his Roman executioners, "Now, at last, I can fulfill the command, 'You shall love the Lord your God with all your heart and all your life.' "

At Yavneh, when discussing the Song of Songs, the other rabbis maintained that it corrupted the minds of youth, citing such lines as, "Oh, give me the kisses of your mouth, for your love is more delightful than wine. Your ointments yield a sweet fragrance. Your name is like finest oil — therefore do maidens love you. Draw me after you, let us run." Akiva, however, looked further, at lines like these:

> Let me be a seal upon your heart,
> Like the seal upon your hand.
> For love is fierce as death,
> Passion is mighty as the grave,
> Its darts are darts of fire,
> A blazing flame.
> Vast floods cannot quench love,
> Nor rivers drown it.
> If a man offered all his wealth for love,
> He would be laughed to scorn.

Akiva sensed the power of love in his own life, and that these moving lyrical verses expressed something of divine importance. He realized that human love is only a metaphor for the love of God. "The Song of Songs is a song of bonding. It is a passionate celebration of the mystical love that flows among God, nature, and humanity, a radical intimacy loosed. It is heard in the mysticism of the earth" (Hirni, *op. cit.*).

During the debate at Yavneh, Akiva arose and said, "God forbid that a Jewish scholar should suggest that Shir HaShirim is not a holy book. Rather, this must be our view: The whole history of the world is not more important than the day on which Shir HaShirim was written. If all the books of the Bible are holy, then Shir HaShirim is the Holy of Holies" (Mishnah, Yadaim 3:5).

Power of Love

Human experience confirms Akiva's views. We read in a story by Tolstoy that an angel who has disobeyed God is punished by being sent, wingless and naked, into the churchyard of a small Russian village. A poor cobbler passing by, ignorant of the angel's divine origin, saves him from freezing to death, gives him food, shelter, and clothing, and keeps him on as an apprentice.

Several years pass. One day, the fallen angel smiles and his face radiates an extraordinarily dazzling light. The cobbler wonders about his guest's origin, and asks about the radiant light around him. The angel reveals himself, and explains that the only way that he will be able to return to Heaven is to learn what people live by. As the story unfolds, it becomes clear that the angel has already taken the first step in becoming a man, when he was rescued from freezing in the churchyard. Now, declares the angel, he has fully realized that human beings cannot live merely each for him or herself — they are necessary to one another, and that *love* is what they live by.

In the modern era, Leo Buscaglia decries the lack of ability to love.

> Our growing inability to relate one with another is reaching frightening proportions. Soon the two-parent family will be considered the exception. Notions of marriage, of extended families and long-lasting friendships are more and more being considered outmoded. Meaningless sexual promiscuity is accepted as the norm and even being advocated as useful behavior for solving problems in failing marriages. Emotional detachment, maintaining our distance from others, is being prescribed as a solution for avoiding pain. Neglect and abuse of children and the aged is a growing problem. Social and religious institutions, which in the past helped to set standards of behavior and brought people together in companionship, are actively downgraded. Individualism, independence, and personal freedom are valued above love, commitment, and cooperation. (Leo Buscaglia, *Loving Each Other*, pp. 12-13.)

Lessons of Love

1. Love is commitment.
   There are several words in the Bible for love. *Ahavah* is one. However, a stronger word is *Hesed*. Scholars of the Jewish Publication Society were translating the Bible, they studied the word *Hesed* carefully, settling on "steadfast love" as the proper translation. *Hesed* is more than *Ahavah*; implying obligation, sentiment, and commitment, it does not depend on how you feel when you wake up in the morning.

   The Prophet Malachi criticizes people for divorcing wives they had taken in their youth. He calls a wife *Havertekha ve'ayshet breetekha* (2:14) - your companion and "covenanted wife." Marriage is love through the covenant. *Hesed* is love that has been solidified and deepened. Today, the marriage ceremony is sometimes cheapened, and to some, it may be just a formality. Others "fall out of love" and feel they must move on to a new partner. Sometimes divorce is necessary, but probably not as often as it occurs today.

2. Love is caring.
   We often confuse romance with real caring.

   The romantic lover indulges himself in love somewhat like a cat. A cat does not caress you; he caresses himself against you. So with the romantic lover. He thinks he is in love with his beloved, but more often he is in love with love; he is enjoying being in love, indulging himself in the joys of romantic love. The object of his love seems to be the beloved but in fact what he is in love with is often an image he himself has projected on the beloved, as on a screen. He is in love with his own creation, with a part of himself. (Dr. Allan Fromme, *The Ability to Love*, p. 246.)

Caring love considers the welfare of the other as much as for the self. When one gets as much satisfaction in the achievements of the other as for himself, then the state of love exists. Deep love brings much reward. It is love that emerges from the center of one's being. It does not depend on responses, recognition/gratitude of others. Rather, it is self-generating and without fear, freeing the people it touches instead of binding them with guilt or expectation. This kind of love is bountiful, rather than exhausting itself on only one person, animal, or object. "It extends itself courageously to the unknown rather than restricting itself to the known." (Ferucci, *What We May Be*, pp. 179ff.)

The other kind of love — from the periphery instead of the center — is basically the love of being loved. Peripheral love expects recognition and support and thus lives in fear of not getting its needs met. Needing immediate gratification, it may be capricious, dictatorial, and impermanent. Conversely, conscious love from the center wishes that the object of one's love should reach its own native perfection, regardless of the consequences to the lover. Love from the center gives the space needed for insight to take place. It protects and strengthens the most delicate elements of our beings. It nourishes our intelligence and our creativity, helps melt our blocks, untie knots, open closures. Love from the center permits us to rediscover our self and motivates us to reach our destiny.

3. Love is service.
Love from the center is service. In other words, service is love in action (Ferucci, p. 184). When we love or serve others, we elicit their resources. We find pleasure by giving. Our love expresses itself in opening our hearts and sharing. By doing so, the other person grows with us. When we serve others, we enlarge our vision, release positive feelings, stimulate creativity, increase self-confidence, have a greater interest in life. We tap our highest energies, and evoke a joyous sense of interdependence on others. We find great release and expansion through loving service.

Love and Pesach

Akiva's insight was powerful: Love is determinative. There is no better time than Pesach to recognize the healing force of love in our lives — the time when families gather at Seder tables, examine values, transmit heritage, share affection and commitment, and express connectedness in the steadfast love *(Hesed)* of the Covenant with God and the Jewish people.

Like Rabbi Akiva, anthropologist and philosopher Ashley Montague realized the potency of love in our lives when he said:

> As a result of our misunderstanding of what we are on this earth for, we have brought ourselves very near to the edge of doom. I regard most people as dead, simply as creatures wandering around, having no realization of why they are on this earth. They have no idea that *the only reason for being on this earth is to live to love!* (Quoted by Herbert Otto, *Love Today*, p. 273.)

May Pesach and our Seder tables remind us that love is what we are all about — Love is what we live by. Love offered from the deep center of our being — offered as true commitment, caring, and honest service — can truly heal the world.

Shir HaShirim asks: "*mee zot olah* . . . Who is this arising like the dawn? Who is this coming up from the wilderness?"

"Standing at the mouth of our cave, out of the sounds of silence, comes our own song of songs:

> May the time of bondage be passing, the wandering be over and gone,
> May the dawning of truth appear on the earth, the season of singing resume,
> And may the voice of justice (and love) be heard in our land."
> (Hirni, *op. cit.*)

IDOLATRY

Are the Ten Commandments outmoded? The Sabbath is ignored or desecrated. Adultery is becoming more commonplace. It is a sorry comment that even the Attorney General of the United States created such a "sleaze factor" that President Bush went out his way to emphasize ethics as important in government.

One commandment we may believe is outmoded is the prohibition against idolatry. However, this belief is erroneous. Idolatry is one of the most serious problems in modern times.

Paul Tillich spoke of the "ultimate concern": everyone needs an object of devotion, something to elicit loyalty and motivate self-investment. This need is so compelling that those who don't find a worthy object of devotion search for one that is unworthy. They devote themselves to a "low object." That, my friends, is idolatry.

In Judaism, nothing short of a growing relationship with God will satisfy one's hunger for an object of ultimate devotion.

The Symbol of Our Age

In the Jewish community, it has been said that materialism has become our God. For example, some years ago, a study of college students asked, "What is the most important thing in your life?" Three-fourths of the Catholic students said, "Living in accordance with my religious beliefs." One-half of the Protestant students replied, "To make the world a better place." One-half of the Jewish students answered, "Economic independence."

Our humor also reflects the values by which our society lives. Consider these examples:

> Cartoon: A lawyer reads a will to the family: "Being of sound mind and body, I spent it all."
> Poster: "Remember the Golden Rule: He who has the gold makes the rules."

Like an addiction, materialism grows until you can't shake it. As the saying goes, "Civilization is the process by which yesterday's luxuries become today's necessities." Our age is one of anxiety, depression, and loneliness. Psychologists tell us that some people shop when they are anxious or depressed, just as others may eat, smoke, or drink. Shopping has become another in a long list of addictions our society is plagued by. But behind this psychological illness lies a spiritual illness — a perversion of values.

During winter break, when my children were home from college, I took them shopping. My son Jonathan's coat had been stolen at a college fraternity party.

I bought him a new coat, and began to list rules for him: don't hang it in the closet at parties, don't take it if you are going to a strange place, etc. Jonathan said to me, "Am I going to own this coat or will it own me?"

The coat was not that expensive, but when my son made this remark, I thought of the women who wear their fur coats to shul and never leave them in the coat closet. They sit in the warm shul for three hours on Shabbat morning with the coat on their laps. This is understandable, but it points out what Harold Wallace Ross, founder of *The New Yorker*, called the "insidious tyranny of things" — the control that our material possessions have over our lives.

In Beachwood, Ohio, a city nearly 95% Jewish, we find one of the most elegant, fancy shopping malls in the Cleveland area. Has shopping become a substitute for religion? For us today, **Beachwood Place** mall is similar to the ancient Temple in Jerusalem for biblical Jews: a central sanctuary, a shrine of worship of our most prized values: economic independence, luxury, ease, and appearance.

We must be examples to our children and teach them the right Jewish and spiritual values. What we need to help our children see is that we need fewer valuables and more values. We must learn to judge people less by their many goods than by their great goodness.

Another Symbol

Beachwood Place mall is one shrine. Two other symbols of the Age of Affluence are funerals and the accompanying shiva. At funerals we witness expensive caskets, which are followed by elaborate "shiva parties."

The Talmud tell us:

> In former times, when food and drink were brought into the house of the mourners, rich people were served out of baskets of silver, while poor people were served out of baskets of willow twigs. The rich drank wine served in precious white glasses, while the poor drank from everyday colored glasses. The deceased of the rich were carried in ornamental stately caskets, while those of the poor were laid out in plain boxes. (*Moed Katan* 27a-b)

All of the above changed through the example of the affluent Rabban Gamliel. The Talmud expresses this powerful refrain: "Because the poor felt shamed, they instituted the practice that all should be treated alike. The rich and the poor were served out of baskets of willow twigs and colored glasses, and buried in plain pine boxes." The Talmud thus teaches us that the blessing of wealth must not be shamed by ostentation and greed.

The Absence of Spirituality

A corollary of the surfeit of materialism is the absence of spirituality. We fill our lives with things because we have not developed an appreciation of higher values — prayer, study, arts, friendship, family, giving, and helping those less fortunate.

Where does happiness come from? We've lost the answer. It does not come from things! A wise person once asked, "How much does it take to make a person happy?" The answer: Just a little more. We are always scraping for just a little more: more money, a bigger house, a better car — something we can show off to others to prove we are "making it." Yet, our lives remain empty as we fill them with *things*. As Carl Sandburg once said, "Money buys everything but love, personality, freedom, immortality, silence, and peace."

Suggestion

Next time you have a decision to make about something new to buy or own, say no. See what happens. Heed the words of Henry David Thoreau, "A man is rich in proportion to the number of things he can do without," and those of Rabbi Pinchas of Koretz, "Rather than possess what I desire, I prefer to desire what I possess." In Pirke Avot we read: "Who is truly rich: one who is content with his lot."

In this vein, a story is told about a woman who visited her friend who lived in a beautiful part of the countryside, but in a very plain shack. Her hostess remarked, "If you should want anything you don't have, just ask for it. We can show you how you can do without it."

President George Bush spoke of materialism in his inaugural address in 1988:

> Are we enthralled with material things, less appreciative of the nobility of work and sacrifice? My friends, we are not the sum of our possessions. They are not the measure of our lives. In our hearts we know what matters. We cannot hope only to leave our children a bigger car, a bigger bank account. We must hope to give them a sense of what it means to be a loyal friends, a loving parent, a citizen who leaves his home, his neighborhood, better than he found it.

The President continued that he hoped he "can celebrate the quieter, deeper successes that are made not of gold and silk, but of better hearts and finer souls."

Let's join our President in helping to make these words come true.

THE UNIVERSAL NEED FOR AFFIRMATION

The need to be affirmed by others has been expounded by prominent humanist psychologists such as Carl Rogers, Abraham Maslow, and others. Part of the process of becoming a happy, whole, and psychologically healthy (mature, self-actualizing) person is to be validated in word and deed by significant others in our phenomenal world (Cf. Elkins, Dov Peretz, *Teaching People to Love Themselves*, Chapter 3, "The Affirmation Model"). Buber's words are relevant here:

> The basis of man's life with man is twofold, and it is one -- the wish of every man to be confirmed as what he is, even as what he can become, by men; and the innate capacity in man to confirm his fellow-men in this way. . . . Man wishes to be confirmed in his being by man, and wishes to have a presence in the being of the other. . . . Secretly and bashfully he watches for a Yes which allows him to be and which can come to him only from one human person to another. (Martin Buber, *The Knowledge of Man*, Harper, 1965.)

If affirmation is a significant contribution, not a demand which tradition places upon us, then disaffirmation, or disvalidation, is forbidden. *Leshon HaRa* (gossip, slander, speaking ill of someone) is the primary negative command which is the Jewish referent of disconfirmation. Speaking ill of another can be understood as one of the primary means in which one's actions redound to the psychological ill-health of his neighbor. In psycho-ethical terms, *Leshon HaRa*, or disaffirmation (disvalidation), undermines God's plan for the human person in his quest to become fully self-actualizing.

Much has been written in Jewish sources on the subject of *Leshon HaRa* and its pernicious effects on the emotional, physical, and spiritual well-being of human beings (see the writings of Chafetz Chaim, for example). Little has been written, however, on two specialized aspects of the subject of affirmation and disaffirmation. The remainder of this paper concerns itself with these two specialized aspects of the subject of affirmation.

Self-Denigration Forbidden

In delineating various aspects of *Leshon HaRa*, the Chafetz Chaim (Rabbi Yisrael Meir HaKohen, 1835-1933) notes that one of the most damaging ways of employing *Leshon HaRa* is on oneself. In other words, one is forbidden to malign, denigrate, or in any way defame one's own name, self, or person. *Leshon HaRa*, the command not to speak ill of persons, thus includes oneself. Yet, students of human nature have long noted that in the guise of humility, many, if not most, people continually malign themselves constantly. We frequently put ourselves down, unwittingly violating the mitzvah of *Leshon HaRa*.

Childhood conditioning leads us to believe that by praising ourselves we evidence lack of humility and are guilty of vanity. We are thus deprived of an important means of self-affirmation. In one study, college students were asked to list all of their positive and negative traits. Results showed that it was far easier to for them to report negative traits. The list of negative attributes was very long, while the list of positive attributes could be counted on one hand. Interestingly, Hasidic tradition informs us that the reason for reciting the *vidui* (Yom Kippur confessional) as an acrostic is to *limit* the negative things we say about ourselves to the 22 letters of the Hebrew alphabet.

Claudio Naranjo, a prominent transpersonal pychotherapist, writes:

> We may see in self-rejection what separates man from part of his experience, deprives him of the knowledge of what or who he is, creates conflicts, and takes away from the freedom to be himself in the surrendering to his own style and calling.
>
> The rejection in the early years of life arrests the individual's growth, and the whole therapeutic process may be seen as one of undoing the resulting self-rejection in order to bring about self-acceptance, self-appreciation, and self-love.
>
> In religious terms, this process can be described as one in which man rediscovers his cosubstantiality with the divine nature, and comes closer to seeing the world and himself as God did on the seventh day of Genesis, when He saw that His creation was good. (Naranjo, *The One Quest*.)

Thus, modern psychology and ancient theology merge on this crucial point: self-denigration is against God's design for the creation of a (psychologically) healthy (whole, holy) human being.

Leshon Ha-Tov: Positivizing the Tradition

Avoiding *Leshon HaRa*, including self-denigration, is only half of the psycho-theological importance of the theme of affirmation. What can be said concerning the positive side of the issue? It is not enough merely to avoid maligning oneself (and others). It is equally important, if not more so, to praise, confirm, affirm, and validate others (and self). Benjamin Franklin once said, "Speak ill of no man, but speak all the good you know of everybody." In this aphorism he captured the full implication of the meaning of human affirmation. Avoid *Leshon HaRa* and go beyond that by affirming and supporting others.

The Torah contains 365 negative commands, and 248 positive commands. Since the majority of these mitzvot are no longer operable, it is not heretical to suggest that we must try in every way possible to make the positive commands in our tradition outweigh the negative ones. In the Torah's great Rebuke (*Tochayha*), in Leviticus 26:14-39 (in Sidrah Be-chukotay), we read of an abundance of curses but only a few blessings. To make this reflect modern understanding of healthy (holy) personality, we must reverse this proportion, and add *berachot* (blessings) as well as reduce *kelalot*. Our model of psychological health is a health- or growth-model, not a disease model. In the spirit of the movement of holistic health, we must help our people grow to greater levels of full personality development, not just avoid the pitfalls of failure, sin, and disease.

In the tradition of Rabbi Abraham Isaac Kook, who added the phrase *Ahavat Hinam* (causeless love) to our vocabulary, in contrast to the negative *Sinat Hinam* (causeless hatred, a Talmudic phrase), I would like to add to our vocabulary the phrase (value concept, in Max Kadushin's words) *Leshon HaTov*: the mitzvah to affirm and confirm others in word and deed, and especially to praise, support and speak well of those around us. We distribute words of praise, appreciation and validation very sparingly. Our stroking is a very limited exercise, often with the express purpose of manipulation. *Leshon HaTov* implies the necessity to praise and validate openly, freely, and abundantly.

In one study on child-rearing practices, a researcher carried a tape-recorder around a house to compare the number of expressions of praise to those of criticism. After compiling data in many households with young children, it became obvious that the common American practice is to offer children one word of praise for every five of criticism. Positive child-rearing practice would suggest reversing that ratio, and insisting that for every expression of criticism there must be five of validation.

Pinchas Peli, writing in the *Jerusalem Post* (July, 1984), makes a relevant comment. Why did Balak, King of Moab, call the foreign prophet, Balaam, to curse Israel? Why, instead of asking him to curse Israel, did he not ask Balaam to bless his own people? Balaam was noted to be very powerful in both blessings and curses (Numbers 22:6). Concludes Professor Peli: "Then, as always, the enemies of Israel preferred its destruction, even at the expense of the destruction of their own peoples, to concentrating on constructive matters which would benefit both themselves and their neighbors." Peli's comments about Israel's enemies can be under- stood as a paradigm for all immature and unevolved persons. They (we) employ the curse, when the blessing is a much more potent weapon.

William James, in his *Varieties of Religious Experience*, taught us that, "The deepest principle in human nature is the craving to be appreciated." Furthermore, "the praise that comes of love does not make us vain, but humble rather," wrote James Barrie, the famous British playwright. There is nothing more soothing to the pained soul than words of support, affirmation, and love. The Torah tells us that when the people of Israel believed "in the Lord and in God's servant Moses," (Exodus 14:31), that is, when the people offered emotional support, through deeds and words, when they affirmed Moses as their leader, "then sang Moses. . . ." Moses was able to sing, to rejoice, when he felt his people's support.

Don't Wait Til It's Too Late

Because we are not acutely aware of the need to affirm each other, we neglect one of life's greatest gifts and one of the most sacred means of creating intimacy. We wait until after death to sing the praises of our beloved ones. When the rabbi visits the house of mourning, in preparation for the writing of a proper eulogy, a family will gather together and pile praise upon praise on their beloved departed. Unfortunately, they often realize only then how wonderful, how life-giving, those sacred words of praise might have been had they been offered during the lifetime of the deceased. How tragic!

A prominent citizen of the community was being given a testimonial dinner. After several lengthy speeches recounting all of his many wonderful contributions to the community, he rose to offer appreciation. "These words of praise sound like a eulogy, except that the corpse is still alive!" Unfortunately, we are so accustomed to hearing words of praise at a funeral, we are ill-at-ease to hear it in front of a living person, when it is so much more appropriate and effective.

In his charming book *Loving Each Other,* Prof. Leo Buscaglia provides another example:

> Several years ago, when I was teaching my Love Class, we decided to attempt an assignment. We agreed to approach those people in our lives whom we valued and loved and express verbally that we "truly loved and appreciated them." We found that what appeared on the surface to be a simple, natural thing was rather more difficult than what we had imagined. Most of the students were lovingly tongue-tied. They felt ill-at-ease, awkward, even embarrassed by expressing their love. Several never completed the assignment. When we discussed and shared our experiences we agreed that it was strange indeed that so many found it threatening to communicate love! It then became obvious why we hear the voice of love so seldom and when it is heard it is spoken so softly, so shyly. This is true even though we have learned that unexpressed love is the greatest cause of our sorrow and regrets. We usually wait until people have died to express their value in our lives, to honor them publicly and to express our love for them. (Leo Buscaglia, *Loving Each Other*. NY: Holt, Rhinehart & Winston, 1984, p. 54).

In the following moving passage, the humanistic psychologist, Clark Moustakas in describes the sorrow he underwent at not being able to inform his late wife in time of the way he felt about her:

> I awoke this morning to a soft and gentle rain, remembering a night not long ago when we paced back and forth while you struggled to come to terms with your dying.

I am writing to tell you how much you have given me in your presence, in your love, in your unqualified acceptance of me. When I came, you always recognized me in a distinctive way. Above all else, I felt I mattered to you. You never let anything -- time, or place or person -- interfere with that. So I have counted on you like the ground I walk on and the air I breathe. You were always there for me in the way the earth and the sky are always there. It simply never occurred to me that the day would come when I would no longer have your eternal faith, that for a while I would lose the earth, the water and the air, that I would have to watch my own footsteps and accept as real the end of a beautiful melody, and of all music.

What grieves me now in this time of painful loneliness is that I never before put my feelings, my sacred valuing of you, into words! In all the other times it was always you who spoke, of how much I offered you, and all the while you were fully there for me. So I want to say clearly and strongly for now and for all the days beyond that you have given me the special gift of life itself, and I know it with my eyes and ears and with all my sense. I will always cherish the unique presence that is you. (*The Touch of Loneliness*, Prentice-Hall, 1975, p. 95).

The Holy Task

Speaking words of praise and affirming others is among the most sacred ways we can facilitate the psychological and spiritual growth of another. It is part of the process of giving birth to a new soul.

George Eliot once warned us, "I like not only to be loved, but to be told that I am loved. The realm of silence is large enough beyond the grave." Mark Twain once said that "I can live on one good compliment for two months."

"Brevity may be the soul of wit," wrote Judith Viorst,

> but not when someone is saying, 'I love you.' When someone's saying 'I love you,' he always ought to give a lot of details: Like Why does he love you? And How much does he love you? And When and Where did he first begin to love you? Favorable comparisons with all the other women he ever loved also are welcome, and even though he insists it would take forever to count the ways, you wouldn't want to discourage him from counting."

Nachum of Chernobyl suggested, based on a line in the *Birkat HaMazon*, that whoever offers words of praise and validation (*b'sorot tovot*) has Elijah the Prophet at his side, and hence hastens the coming of Messiah.

Whether our vocabulary be psychological or spiritual, the transmission of words of love is a holy task and one of the highest of all mitzvot. "Let the people realize clearly," wrote Abraham Maslow,

> that every time they threaten someone or humiliate or hurt unnecessarily or dominate or reject another human being, they become forces for the creation

of psychopathology, even if these be small forces. Let them recognize that every man who is kind, helpful, decent, psychologically democratic, affectionate, and warm, is a psychotherapeutic force even though a small one.

Our task, if we are to realize our highest calling in offering love, care and support to our co-travellers on Spaceship Earth, is to fulfill the positive command of *motzee shem tov* — enhancing the positive reputation of others.

LESHON HA-TOV: A GREAT MITZVAH

In one of his novels, the Russian author Turgenev presents the following dialogue:

> I was once walking in the street when a beggar stopped me. He was a frail old man, with inflamed eyes, blue chapped lips, filthy rough rags and disgusting sores. Oh how poverty had disfigured this repulsive creature!
>
> He stretched out to me his red, swollen, filthy hand and whimpered for alms. I reached into my pocket, but no wallet, no coins, no money did I find. I had left them all at home.
>
> The beggar waited, and his outstretched hand twitched and trembled slightly. Embarrassed and confused I seized his hand and pressed it and said: "Brother, don't be angry with me. I am sorry but I have nothing to give you. I left my wallet at home, brother."
>
> The beggar raised his bloodshot eyes to mine. His blue lips smiled and he returned the pressure of my fingers. "Never mind," he stammered. "Thank you, thank you for this, for this too was a gift. No one ever called me brother before."

It's a touching slice of narrative through which we see a whole lifetime: a beggar who has probably been mistreated and deprived of love most of his life, hungry, tired, desperate for a handout, a few simple coins, and he doesn't even get that. What he does receive is much more valuable. How simple it is to call one our brother or sister, to express a word of love or support to one in emotional need. Yet we rush through life, eyes narrowly focused on the task, hurrying to finish our chores, afraid to take the emotional risk of opening ourselves up to our neighbor, and the kind word goes unexpressed.

In the Great Confessional of Yom Kippur, we list many sins, one of which states, "*Al chet she-chatanu lefanecha bedibbur peh*" — for the sin we have committed before You by the words of our mouths. Sometimes that sin is the expression of a negative word, a nasty comment, a harsh phrase, a cruel joke, or a sarcastic remark. At other times that sin is committed by refraining from a positive remark. Benjamin Franklin reminded us that there are two sides to the power of speech when he wrote, "Speak ill of no man, but speak all the good you know of everybody."

Our tradition uses the phrase *Leshon Ha-Ra* to refer to evil speech — slander, gossip, put-downs, vilification of any kind — a nasty, evil, and pernicious act that can destroy a reputation and ruin a life. One fourth of all the sins listed in the Great Confessional touch on *Leshon Ha-Ra*. However, the other side of the coin is equally important: what I choose to call *Leshon Ha-Tov*.

Leshon Ha-Tov means verbal affirmation of another person, the careful use of words which our tradition implies when it warns us about the sins of speech, of *dibbur peh*. It is what the ancient Greek writer, Cicero, referred to when he said that "the sweetest of all sound is praise."

Affirm Others

Sometimes we are afraid to praise others. We think praise will go to their heads, or that they will be embarrassed. Yet if we think about it carefully, we could wish that we were as careful about praise and compliments as we are careless about gossip and put-downs. No one I know ever died from being appreciated. But many people have been saved from despair and hopelessness by a kind word properly spoken.

The Book of Proverbs, one of the finest collections of wisdom regarding human relationships, contains sage aphorisms about the importance of words of encouragement:

> Pleasant words are like a honeycomb,
> Sweet to the palate and cure for the body. (16:24)

> Care in the heart of a man bows it down
> But a good word makes it glad. (12:25)

> Do not withhold good from one who deserves it
> When you have the power to say it. (3:27)

In the last chapter of the biblical book we find the *Eshet Chayil*, that beautiful poem of praise recited by devoted husbands each Friday night at the Shabbat dinner table, in which we read: "The children of the woman of valor rise up and call her blessed, and her husband praises her, saying, 'Many women have done well, but you surpass them all.'" (31:28, 29)

In the prayers chanted in the daily *Shacharit* service, a selection from Exodus is quoted (14:31): "And when Israel saw the wondrous power which the Lord had wielded against the Egyptians, the people feared the Lord, and they had faith in the Lord and His servant Moshe." The verse continues, "Then sang Moshe," which, the commentaries explain, means that only when the people had faith in Moshe could he sing.

Turgenev's beggar lacked a song in his life because no one had faith in him. Only when we feel the faith, trust, and encouragement of loved ones can we continue our important tasks and achieve our highest potential. There is something powerful in the praise and appreciation of significant people in our lives that holding it back becomes one of the most harmful wedges in any relationship. "The supreme happiness in life," wrote Victor Hugo, "is the conviction that we are loved." *Al chet she-chatanu lefanecha bedibbur peh* --

for the sin which we committed before you with our mouths. The words which we say, and the words we refrain from saying.

Affirmation is an Attitude

What I am saying about words of affirmation and appreciation sounds reasonable enough. So why do we not offer them more frequently? A good psychologist would find many reasons. One of them is that our words are a reflection of our attitude toward people. If our attitudes are positive and constructive, then we will have less difficulty expressing affirmation and praise. In addition, to be happier in their relationships people need to "catch people" doing right more often. This tendency of looking for the good in life and in people will assist us in expressing nice things. We say only what we first see. If we see the good, we will better be able to express it.

Our tradition is full of examples of the need to look positively at others. Several centuries ago, Maimonides addressed this concept in the *Mishneh Torah* (code of Jewish Law): "A wise person gives everyone a friendly greeting, judges all people favorably, loves peace and strives for it, so that all are kindly toward him. He dwells on the merits of his fellow man, without ever disparaging him" (Sefer Hamada 5:7).

To the Hasidic masters, the only way to look upon the another Jew was to do so with a positive mental attitude, and to judge others *le-chaf zechut* — with a presumption of merit. The classic illustration of a positive attitude is that of Rabbi Levi Yitzchak of Berditchev. One Yom Kippur, Reb Levi saw a fellow Jew smoking a cigarette. "Surely," said the Rabbi, "you have forgotten that this is Yom Kippur!" No, said the man, I know that today is Yom Kippur. "Surely," continued Reb Levi, "you are not aware that the Jewish law codes forbid smoking on Yom Kippur." No, said the man, I know that it is forbidden to smoke on Yom Kippur. "Then surely," pursued Reb Levi Yitzchak, "your doctor told you that because of your nerves, you have to smoke on Yom Kippur." No, continued the Jew, I know it's Yom Kippur, I know I shouldn't smoke on Yom Kippur, my doctor did not advise me to smoke, I'm just smoking! "What a wonderful Jew," reacted Reb Levi, "three times I gave him a chance to lie, and he still tells the truth!"

Another story is told of a wealthy Hasid, a diamond merchant, who was listening to his rebbe, Shalom Ber of Lubavitch, praising some of the townspeople. "But Rebbe," argued the Hasid, "why do you make such a fuss over these simpletons?" "Because they have many special qualities," answered the teacher." "Well, I just can't see them," responded the Hasid. Later in the discussion, the rebbe asked to see some of the Hasid's precious diamonds. The gem merchant was delighted to have the opportunity to impress his teacher, and, pointing to a particularly valuable stone, he said to the rebbe, "This one is something really special!" "But I can't see anything in it," said the rebbe. The gem merchant explained to his teacher, "You must be a connoisseur to know how to look at diamonds." The rebbe then said, "But every person is also truly something special. You just have to be a connoisseur to know how to look at him!"

Rabbi Israel Salanter, well-known founder of the Musar Movement (the 19th century effort to center people's attention on ethical responsibilities), explains that God gave us two eyes so that with one we can look at our neighbor, focusing on virtues, and with the other, we are to turn inward to see our own shortcomings in order to correct them.

Family First

The most tragic thing about our failure to affirm is that this happens most with those who most need our affirmation: our family. No one needs love, attention, and appreciation more than a child from a parent, a wife from her husband, a husband from his wife. Yet somehow the family is where we fail most often. Every rabbi has stories of funerals at which he/she officiates, and during which time he/she praises the deceased with the fitting words of a eulogy. Then, someone in the family approaches and says, "You know, Rabbi, there were so many times when I wanted to say words of kindness and love, but I just could not get them out of my mouth." In the words of George Eliot, "I like not only to be loved, but to be told that I am loved; the realm of silence is large enough beyond the grave."

We neglect our children the same way. Children need encouragement and positive reinforcement for their normal growth and development. They need it the same way they need proper nutrition to make their bones get stronger and their bodies grow properly. What William James said over a half a century ago applies with no more force than it does to our children: "The deepest principle of human nature is the craving to be appreciated."

One of the most beautiful customs in our tradition is the blessing by parents of their children on Shabbat eve and before Kol Nidre on Yom Kippur eve. We know that our children do many things that anger and frustrate us. Yet when it comes to the Shabbat blessing, we put aside those negative feelings, and turn our thoughts and words only to pleasant prayers and positive hopes. In the Torah, when both Isaac and Jacob bless their children (Genesis 27:1, 48:10), we are told that "the eyes of the aging patriarch were dimmed for age, so that they could not see." Why, ask the commentators, is it said of both that their eyes are dimmed? This is to inform us that when blessing our children, we should shut our eyes and not see their flaws, only their good points (Cf. Shmuel Yosef Agnon, *Days of Awe*, p. 171).

Psychologist Erik Erikson warns us that "the most deadly of all sins is the mutilation of a child's spirit." An ancient Chinese proverb tell us that a child's life is like a piece of paper on which every passerby leaves a mark. We can add that the mark of a parent is the most potent of all.

Somehow, when relationships are most strongly solidified, such as with family members, it is hardest to break through that emotional barrier and share our deepest feelings of love and caring. While accomplishing this goal requires the most courage, the satisfaction is greatest. Nowhere are acts of affirmation more desperately needed to produce healthy marriages, children, and families than in the home.

It's Okay to be Affirmed

One of the barriers we must transcend in the process of learning how to offer love and appreciation is to accept that we all need such affirmation. Needing others to care about us is not a sign of weakness or immaturity; rather, it is a deep universal human need, and the sooner we recognize it, the easier it will be to accept praise from others. From time to time we discover that some strong, powerful, or heroic figure exposes his or her own personal need for appreciation, and it touches us. We are touched because we (wrongly) assumed all along that strong people did not have these needs.

After President Lincoln's assassination, a number of items were found in his pockets, including eight newspaper clippings lauding his accomplishments. The historian reporting this comments, "Here was a man who withstood brutal verbal abuse without flinching, but when he found an article that praised him, he kept it. Even to a casual reader these eight articles are heart-warming. . . . The contents of Lincoln's pockets have an immediacy that transcends time. They invoke a sad, thoughtful and even vulnerable man." (*NY Times*, 3-29-86)

To all those who believe that praise and appreciation only serve to make one vain, think of Abe Lincoln. Rather than make one vain, *Leshon Ha-Tov* sustains us, uplifts us, and strengthens us. In the words of the British playwright, James Barrie, "The praise that comes of love does not make us vain, but humble rather."

God, Too, Loves Praise

For skeptics who are still unconvinced that the goal of affirming our loved ones is valid, we have one more important piece of evidence. Turn through the leaves of the sacred Book of Psalms and you will find that praise of God is one of the highest forms of prayer. Not only does the Psalmist urge our frequent and melodious praise of God, but God Himself, in the 50th Psalm, asks for it, in these words: "Whoever offers me thanks and praise, honors me" (Psalm 50:23).

The prominent Christian theologian C.S. Lewis asks the obvious question: Why is there so much praise of God in the Psalms? He explains that for a long time he had a hard time accepting the idea that God was so vain so as to ask for compliments from His creatures. Finally, he realized why.

> The world rings with praise . . . readers [praising] their favourite poet, walkers praising the countryside, players praising their favourite game — praise of weather, wines, dishes, actors, motors, horses, colleges. . . . I had not noticed how the humblest, and at the same time most balanced and capacious, minds praised most, while the cranks, misfits and malcontents praised least. . . .
>
> I had not noticed either that just as men spontaneously praise whatever they value, so they spontaneously urge us to join them in praising it: "Isn't she lovely? Wasn't it glorious? Don't you think that magnificent?" The Psalmists in telling everyone to praise God are doing what all men do when they speak of what they care about. . . . I think we delight to praise what we enjoy because the praise not merely expresses but completes the enjoyment; it is its appointed consummation. It is not out of compliment that lovers keep on telling one another how beautiful they are; the delight is incomplete till it is expressed. (C.S. Lewis, *Reflections on the Psalms*)

In sum, if we love, then we must praise that which we love. If we do not love, then we are dead, spiritually if not physically. Giving and receiving unconditional love are the sum of all that we are, and by doing so we affirm those whom we love in the deepest possible way. It is the heart of who we are as human beings and as creatures of God.

May God always give us the gift, and the strength to use it: to love, to share, and to receive, and thus to enlarge our hearts and our capacity for a fuller and deeper life.

THE CHUTZPAH CONTROVERSY

Harvard law professor Alan Dershowitz, international champion of human rights, civil liberties, and Jewish dignity, has written a very controversial book whose theme is summed up in its title: *Chutzpah*. Jews need more assertiveness, more political activism, more temerity in preserving the Jewish People. When Dershowitz spoke recently at the Front Row Theatre in Cleveland, his main thrust was to articulate an important agenda for the Jewish people: fighting anti-Semitism.

The part of Dershowitz's speech that I liked most of all was the following: "The cement of anti-Semitism that has kept us together for so many years is not enough. We have to plan for success. Do we want the epitaph of Judaism to read: 'It was a wonderfully adaptive religion during times of crisis and tragedy, but it failed us when we succeeded. We didn't know how to use it to persuade our children of its positive aspects." (*Cleveland Plain Dealer*, 11-2-91, p. 4E). During the question and answer period following his presentation, I asked him, "What positive program do you follow to assure the success of a solid Jewish future for our children?"

Dershowitz's answer was quite unsatisfying. He said that each person must find his own way, which is easy to agree with, and that his way was through political activism. This is fine, but not enough. In addition, I fear that for far too many people, fighting anti-Semitism is the be-all and end-all of Jewish existence. Is anti-Semitism the only thing that pushes some people to shout their pride in their Jewish faith and heritage? Anti-anti-Semitism is not enough!

Dershowitz tells a story related to him by novelist Herman Wouk, an Orthodox Jew. While in Cracow working on the TV version of his book, *War and Remembrance,* Wouk put on his *tallit* and *tefillin* one morning, as he did daily. Later that morning, he visited a small Jewish Museum where he saw a pair of *tefillin* under a glass cover, with the following legend: "These are *tefillin* which used to be worn by Jews while they prayed." Dershowitz continues: "Herman (Wouk) told me how it struck him with special power precisely because he had just finished praying with his *tefillin*. I responded that the story had even greater impact on me because I was one of those Jews who *used* to wear *tefillin* when I prayed every day."

The next sentence struck me as particularly interesting. "I was — am — one of those Jews, as are my children, who are making the museum case statement come true. If anything could drive me back to *tefillin*, it would not be religious conviction; it would be a political desire to fight those who want to see Judaism and Jews relegated to interesting museum exhibits and poignant memorials."

Chutzpah, Nachas, and the Next Generation

In truth, besides encouraging political activism, Dershowitz has done very little to pass on the heritage of Judaism to his children. I get the impression that his children are very assimilated and don't have anywhere near the commitment to Judaism, the Jewish People, and Jewish learning that their father has (he attended Yeshivah for 12 years and is a knowledgeable Jew). What about the next generation? Is his kind of Judaism strong enough, deep enough, to preserve what he received from his parents and pass it on to his children? It seems doubtful. Dershowitz is like a beautifully smelling flower, plucked from its roots. It still gives off a beautiful scent, but cannot reproduce itself. It is cut off from its past, and has no future.

I only wish that the title of Dershowitz's book were not *Chutzpah*, but *Nachas*. Maybe it would not have sold as many copies, because "nachas" is not as well-known a term as "chutzpah." The world respects and admires the Jewish People today for its **chutzpah**, for its courage in recreating its national existence in the State of Israel after 2000 years of exile. Chutzpah is an admirable trait, at least the way Dershowitz uses it. To him, it means assertiveness, standing up for one's rights, a quality which has helped keep the Jewish People alive. Doubtless we need for much more of it today, as he so eloquently explains in his book. But it simply doesn't go far enough. Chutzpah bereft of Jewish knowledge and spirituality is an empty shell. It is arrogance, not courage; defensiveness, not pride; reactive, not proactive. Unless chutzpah includes nachas, true Jewish satisfaction in being a knowledgeable Jew, it is not really a commodity that will win the hearts and souls of the next generation.

Chutzpah is important for Jews with a background like that of Dershowitz: 12 years in a yeshiva, where he studied Bible, Talmud, Jewish philosophy, Jewish history, and the Hebrew language. As an educated Jew, he can therefore be a proud, self-respecting Jew. He can fight for the Jewish People, because he knows what and for whom he is fighting. Sadly, his children don't know that! They only know that it's important to fight to protect Jews, human rights, and civil liberties. But who are these strange Jews, and what is their unique heritage that demands they fight for it? I don't think his children really know, and when the battle is over and won, what is left? What will sustain them? Dershowitz asks the right question, but he just doesn't give any adequate answer. His own life doesn't provide an answer, and I am afraid that he and his children will continue to be Jews who testify to the truth of the museum statement:

> Jews are a people who *used to* wear tefillin! Jews are a people who *used to* keep Shabbat! Jews are a people who *used to* pray! Jews are a people who *used to* study about their history and their culture!

Jews are a people who *used to* know who they were, and were proud of their identity because it was part of their daily existence, in more ways than just fighting off the enemy. They will crawl out of the woodwork and scream to the rooftops their pride in being Jewish when the Arabs cross the borders of Israel with their tanks, or when someone says God doesn't hear the prayers of Jews, or when a KKK member runs for Governor of Louisiana, or when Cardinal Glemp says that the Jews made the Poles into alcoholics. When that happens, Alan, Elon, and Jamin Dershowitz will jump to their feet and fight the good battle, defend our honor, protect us, and help save us.

But for what?

Why fight the battle? Why preserve the Jewish people, if all we know is fighting off the "goyim"? Dershowitz is absolutely right when he says that it is simply not enough! For 4000 years the mission of the Jewish people has not been to stay the enemy from our doors, but to be a kingdom of priests and a holy nation. Being Jewish can't only be for fighting for Russian Jews, Ethiopian Jews, or Israeli Jews, though that is, of course, very important. We need a positive program. It doesn't matter what helps you preserve Jewish culture, be it *tefillin*, Torah study, Shabbat, prayer, Hanukkah, or Jewish songs, or all of the above. A positive program produces the kind of feeling that Judaism is a tradition that can save us during times of peace as well as times of war.

The Real Battle is with Ourselves

Jews face an uphill battle most of the time. We need a lot of chutzpah, self-esteem, and nachas to fight the battle. However, the most important battle Jews must fight is not against the enemy without, but rather the enemy within: apathy, ignorance, assimilation, intermarriage, and Jewish self-hatred. The real battle is against our own spiritual weakness and the self-inflicted wounds of letting Judaism sit under a glass in a museum, instead of living it every day of our lives.

As long as Jewish education is a step-child in Jewish life; as long as the synagogue is on the bottom of the ladder of Jewish priorities in the Jewish community; as long as Jewish books lie on the shelves unread; as long as Jewish prayer is only for the rabbi and hazzan; as long as our charity dollars are lavish for old ages homes and Holocaust Museums and lectures to churches and Christians — and stingy when it comes to the preservation of the Jewish heritage, culture and religion, then we haven't earned the right to act with chutzpah. We don't really need chutzpah, because there is no need to fight a battle unless you know why you're fighting. But when we live Judaism every day, then chutzpah can be the most wonderful quality any human being ever had.

A century ago, Czar Nicholas of Russia and Emperor Franz Joseph of Austria argued over treatment of the Jews. The Czar just couldn't understand why his Austrian counterpart was giving freedom and civil rights to Austrian Jews. The Czar claimed that his way of dealing with the Jews was much more befitting this unworthy people — decimate them with pogroms and persecution. "Dear Czar," said Franz Joseph, "you kill your Jews your way, and I'll kill my Jews my way."

If Jews survive into the 21st century, it will not be because we were able to fight off the anti-Semitism of the Czar, Stalin, Hafez el Asad, or Saddam Hussein, though I am fully in agreement that they must be fought and defeated. Rather, it will be because we did not let Franz Joseph sit and gloat while the Jewish people destroyed itself from within.

We need chutzpah today not for fighting anti-Semitism but for preserving Judaism. We need not just a league for anti-defamation but a league for philo-Judaism. We need not only outreach, but in-reach. To survive today we must not only ward off the swastika painters and Jew-baiters, but also strengthen every institution which promotes Jewish pride and helps us be a kingdom of priests and a holy nation.

Like our cartoon friend, Pogo, I am afraid that we have discovered the real enemy of the Jewish People, and it is us. That idea may be hard to swallow, and you may think it's chutzpah of me to say so, but it's the only kind of chutzpah I know of that can keep us going for another 4000 years!

Part II:

Judaism for the New Age

SHABBAT AS FANTASY

On Rosh HaShanah I made a case for the concept in Judaism that holiness and morality, ritual and ethics, are inextricably intertwined, and that the ultimate goal of Judaism is to train and educate Jews, to be compassionate, sensitive, caring, menschen — people with a heart. Today, Yom Kippur, I carry that argument further by giving you the best example I know of how Judaism is a system of Holiness and Morality bound together. I'll tell you what that example is in a few minutes.

Since this is the holiest day in the Jewish calendar — and since I have a most passionate urge to get my message across this evening more than I ever have before, I want you to cooperate with me in a novel experiment.

l want you to use your imagination as I speak, and visualize the scene I paint for you. If you will do this for me, then my words will have a much better chance of reaching you. If I were a practitioner of some esoteric cult, you might be reluctant to participate in a psychological experiment, but I assure you that this is not a figment of your imagination — this is your Rabbi speaking to you, and I don't want you to give up all your worldly possessions and come live in my ashram. I merely want you to feel what I have to say very deeply, and take it home with you in your memory and in your heart, and discuss it with your family and friends, and let it simmer in your soul for some time. I hope you will visualize a picture with the potential to bring you better health, more serenity, a more closely knit family, deeper emotional security, lots of beauty in the way of art, music, poetry, and a feeling of being closer to God. All that at once. It's worth giving it a try, isn't it?

The Journey

Picture yourself in a small European shtetl, a little village totally inhabited by your fellow Jews, some time in the 19th century. It's Thursday afternoon, and all week, since last Saturday night, you've been waiting for this time to come closer, closer to Shabbat. You go to the market to shop for Shabbat dinner, and bring home the very best foods available. Since chicken is a great delicacy for you, that's the main course. You buy all of the other delectable foods you relish for your loving family and bring them home.

The next morning, Friday, if you are the wife, you begin to clean the house (as women did in Eastern Europe), and if you are the husband, you are chopping wood for the Shabbat fire, or picking the most beautiful flowers for the Shabbat table, or helping with the cleaning around the house for the special guest, the Shabbat bride, who will soon be coming.

Now it's late Friday afternoon, and everyone has bathed. The table is set beautifully, as befits a Sabbath-observing family. Silver goblets embellish the table, brim-full of delicious sweet crimson wine, and the freshly baked challahs are golden, warm and soft. The mood is serene and hushed. An unusual and special quiet descends on the home, an inner peacefulness and joy. The past six days have been filled with hard work, much accomplishment, frantic business, and now the world is slowing down on its axis, and spinning a bit more gently and gradually.

As the sun begins to fade in the sky, its red ball of fire is sinking behind the leaves and branches of the trees, and the sky is a mixture of gray, blue and orange, with a few puffs of white clouds dotting the horizon. Without the warm rays of the sun beaming through the window of your home, it's getting colder, and the family snuggles together to provide warmth. Mother approaches the beautiful golden candelabra, handed down to her from her mother and grandmother, which has room for five candles, one for each member of the family. Just as she is about to light the Shabbat candles, Papa enters the house with a guest — a stranger in town. For after all, what is Shabbat without a guest at the table? He is an itinerant merchant who found himself far from home on Shabbat. So he went to the local shul, and when he started to leave at the end of services, several men approached him to invite him to come home with them for dinner. Papa, you were the first to reach him, and he accepted your invitation.

For the next few moments of our story, let me read to you a personal account in a poem by Philip Raskin, called, "Kindling the Sabbath Light"

> From memory's spring flows a vision tonight;
> My mother is kindling and blessing the light.
>
> The light of queen Sabbath, the heavenly flame
> That one day in seven quells hunger and shame.
>
> My mother is praying, and screening her face,
> Too bashful to gaze at the Sabbath light's grace.
>
> She murmurs devoutly: "Almighty, be blessed
> For sending Thy angel of joy and of rest.
>
> And may, as the candles of Sabbath divine,
> The eyes of my son in Thy Law ever shine"...
>
> Of childhood, fair childhood, the years are long fled;
> Youth's candles are quenched, and my mother is dead.
>
> And yet ev'ry Friday, when twilight arrives,
> The face of my mother within me revives;
>
> A prayer on her lips: "O Almighty, be blessed

>For sending us Sabbath, the angel of rest."
>
>And some hidden feelings I cannot control
>A Sabbath light kindles deep, deep in my soul.

Continuing our Shabbat imagery now, Papa then blesses the children, with his hands resting gently and lovingly on their heads, and plants a soft kiss on their cheeks when he is finished. Next he reads the loving poem of praise to his *eshet chayil,* his woman of valor — whose worth is far above rubies, and who exceeds all other women in her qualities of generosity and piety.

Papa then chants the *kiddush,* in which he praises God for sanctifying the Shabbat, a day of rest recalling God's own rest after the six days of creation, and reminding us of God's command that every person be as liberated as the people who left Egyptian slavery. Only a free person can enjoy a Shabbat; a slave cannot appreciate the meaning of rest, or of freedom or Shabbat. The challah has been covered, so that the innocent challah would not be offended by seeing that the wine was blessed first. Papa removes the cover and picks up the two shiny home-baked loaves, the double portion reminding the family of the double measure of joy they are to celebrate on the Sabbath, and thanks God with the *motzee* for the privilege of having such sumptuous food on the table, at least this once during the week.

After dinner the family revels in singing some Shabbat *z'mirot,* Sabbath hymns, together, as they linger at the table in great leisure. There is nowhere to go, no appointments to rush to. They have only to satisfy their physical appetites for food, drink, song, and relaxation. When mama and papa finally go to bed, they have a double mitzvah for having sexual relations that night, for it is a great mitzvah to enjoy each other's physical and spiritual love on Shabbat. Shabbat is a mitzvah, and sex is a mitzvah, but sex on Shabbat is literally an embarrassment of riches.

Values Inherent in Shabbat

Our reverie is now complete, and you may awaken, if you wish. Or, if you prefer, instead of listening to the rest of the sermon, if you are really totally immersed in the scene in which you joined me in your mind's eye, then you may remain there, and someone else will tell you about the rest of my message, because the picture in your head is indeed worth a thousand sermons.

For those of you who are more cerebrally oriented, and wish to analyze with me the painting we just sketched together, I want to give you a few explanations of what Shabbat does for me in my life, and for the people I know who keep it somewhat faithfully.

1) First, keeping Shabbat brings *dignity* to our life.
Our lives lack humanity. We often feel like automatons, like machines, going

through the motions. We listen to our boss, do our work, carpool the kids, "religiously" follow what our computerized calendar tells us to do from hour to hour, run from party to party, movie to movie, event to event, meeting to meeting. Look at the faces of people waiting for a commuter train and you will see the trouble with our frenetic motion: there is a blank, hollow and sometimes even bitter look on their faces. The same is true of the people I see about 7 in the morning as I am doing my daily 2 miles around the block, driving by in their Mercedes or Cadillacs, busy giving orders on the phone to someone waiting at the office to which they cannot arrive too quickly.

Shabbat reminds us that we are not slaves, but free people. Free to choose a life of sanctity and specialness, not just to stay on the treadmill and try to race as fast as the people in front of you or behind you.

My colleague Rabbi Samuel Dresner has written:

> The real purpose of life is not to conquer nature but to conquer the self; not to fashion a city out of a forest but to fashion a soul out of a human being; not to build bridges but to build human kindness; not to learn to fly like a bird or swim like a fish but to walk on the earth like a man; not to erect skyscrapers but to establish mercy and justice; not to manufacture an ingenious technical civilization but to be holy in the midst of unholiness. The real tasks are to learn how to remain civilized in the midst of insanity; how to retain a share in man's dignity in the midst of the Dachaus and Buchenwalds, how to keep the mark of Cain from obscuring the image of the divine, how to fashion a home of love and peace, how to create children obedient and reverent, how to find the strength to perform the *mitzvot*, how to bend our will to God's will.

2) Second, Shabbat offers us a way to keep *Jewishness* in our home, in our family, and in our own personal life.
In ancient times the Greeks called the Jews lazy, because they took off one day in seven, absenting themselves from productive labor. When you think about it, a traditional Jew spends 1/7 of his life not engaged in gainful employment. To the Greeks that was a sin! If you live to be 70, you will have observed 10 years of Shabbat! Imagine!

We must remember, however, that the glory of ancient Greece is gone, and the Jewish People survives. The Sabbath has been our portable sanctuary. More than the Jewish People kept the Sabbath, a 19th century philosopher reminds us, the Sabbath kept us alive as a people!

> Chaim Nachman Bialik, the great Hebrew poet, tells a beautiful story of how his family when cruelly deported from its home in Tsarist Russia, found itself desolately and aimlessly wandering in a forest. Suddenly, his mother realized that it was Friday afternoon and as sunset was approaching, she immediately pulled out from somewhere two little candles, lit them, covered her face to recite the blessing over the Sabbath and all at once 'we were back home again.' Between the stars flickering above and the Sabbath candles flickering below,

they no longer felt uprooted and ashamed. While probably realizing subconsciously that the Sabbath was bound inevitably to come to an end, they were, for the time being, in a peaceful, serene (and Jewish) home. (Pinchas Peli, *Shabbat Shalom*, p. 81).

3) Third, the Shabbat gives us *a set of values* and imposes a template of meaning on our life.

Shabbat gives our table conversation a framework of depth when we talk of the weekly Sidrah (Torah portion). It carries us away to our own private island of peace and serenity, which no one, not even a cruel dictator, or a relentless computer, can take away from us, because it exists in our own mind.

Rabbi Abraham Joshua Heschel once asked an interesting question. If God could create beautiful mountains, and flowing rivers, and stately trees, and a sunset and sunrise that take our breath away, why did the Almighty not create for us Jews — God's chosen people — a synagogue, a sanctuary? Heschel's answer: God did create a sanctuary. But not a sanctuary in space. He created a sanctuary in *time*. Other religions sanctified things of space, while Judaism sanctified time. Only time, and people, are holy; things cannot be holy in the deepest sense. To make physical objects holy is a kind of fetish. The Shabbat, wrote Heschel, is our sanctuary in time.

The Shabbat reminds us that we are adherents of a faith which sanctifies time instead of space; it favors *being* in place of *doing*; it prefers loving people to using them. All of this is what Shabbat comes to teach us.

4) Fourth, Shabbat has a benefit which borders between the psychological and the spiritual.

Because we can only reach that deep plane of true spirituality if our mind is at ease and our ego is firm. Let me teach you a Shabbat law: it is forbidden to worry on the Sabbath day. Did you know that?

When the Bible dictates that we are to finish all our work in six days, and rest on the seventh day, the rabbis ask: How can we really finish all our work in six days? Surely there will be more left for next week?! Naturally, they answer their own question: Of course, you cannot finish all your work, but on the Shabbat, you must act and think as if all your work were completed. Don't let a thought of it enter your mind; don't let it disturb your Shabbat Menuchah, your Sabbath rest.

Do you remember the popular song by Bobby McPheran, "Don't Worry, Be Happy"? Maybe it sold millions of copies because it reminded people who are frantically searching for a day in their lives when they can let go of their worries, relax, and just be happy. We all need a day each week to allow ourselves to smell the flowers, and enjoy the fruits of God's glorious creation.

So it's forbidden to worry on the Shabbat. If the letter carrier brings you bills on Shabbat, you don't open them. If the yard needs mowing or the fence needs fixing, it is forbidden on Shabbat, so you can't worry about it. If you have an unsolved problem at work, leave it there Friday afternoon, and it will still wait for you on Monday morning. For Heaven's sake, don't take it home with you! Be happy, don't worry! For if you take home your worries, you'll spoil your Shabbat.

Herman Wouk, an Orthodox Jew, author of the *Winds of War, War and Remembrance,* and other novels, also who wrote a book about Judaism, *This is My God*. In the chapter about Shabbat, Wouk describes the tension and pressure, as well as the excitement and pleasure, that take place in the days before a play he authored opens on Broadway. Here are Wouk's own words:

> Friday afternoon, during these rehearsals, inevitably seems to come when the project is tottering on the edge of ruin. I have sometimes felt guilty of treason, holding to the Sabbath in such a desperate situation. But then, experience has taught me that a theatre enterprise almost always is in such a case. Sometimes it does totter to ruin, and sometimes it totters to great prosperity, but tottering is its normal gait, and cries of anguish are its normal tone of voice. So I have reluctantly taken leave of my colleagues on Friday afternoon, and rejoined them on Saturday night. The play has never yet collapsed in the meantime. When I return I find it tottering as before, and the anguished cries as normally despairing as ever. My plays have encountered in the end both success and failure, but I cannot honestly ascribe either result to my observing the Sabbath.
>
> Leaving the gloomy theatre, the littered coffee cups, the jumbled scarred-up scripts, the haggard actors, the shouting stagehands, the bedevilled director, the knuckle-gnawing producer, the clatttering typewriter, and the dense tobacco smoke and backstage dust, I have come home. It has been a startling change, very like a brief return from the wars. My wife and my boys, whose existence I have almost forgotten in the anxious shoring up of the tottering ruin, are waiting for me, gay, dressed in holiday clothes, and looking to be marvelously attractive. We have sat down to a splendid dinner, at a table graced with flowers and the old Sabbath symbols: the burning candles, the twisted loaves, the stuffed fish, and my grandfather's silver goblet brimming with wine. I have blessed my boys with the ancient blessing: we have sung the pleasantly syncopated Sabbath table hymns. The talk has had little to do with totering ruins. My wife and I have caught up with our week's conversation. The boys, knowing that the Sabbath is the occasion for asking questions, have asked them. The Bible, the encyclopedia, the atlas, have piled up on the table. We talk of Judaism, and there are the usual impossible boys' queries about God, which my wife and I field clumsily but as well as we can. For me it is a retreat into restorative magic.
>
> Saturday has passed in much the same manner. The boys are at home in the synagogue, and they like it. They like even more the assured presence of their parents. In the weekday press of schooling, household chores and work - and especially in a play-producing time — it often happens that they see little of us. On the Sabbath we are always there, and they know it. They know too that I

am not working, and that my wife is at her ease. It is their day.

It is my day, too. The telephone is silent. I can think, read, study, walk, or do nothing. It is an oasis of quiet. When night falls, I go back to the wonderful nerve-racking Broadway game. Often I make my best contribution of the week then and there to the grisly literary surgery that goes on and on until opening night. My producer one Saturday night said to me, "I don't envy you your religion, but I envy you your Sabbath."

5) Fifth, Shabbat is a time for *family*.

God knows that today our families are in desperate need of help — any kind of help. Someone once described the Shabbat in an ideal Jewish home as a place where warmth rules over technology. A Hasidic rabbi explained it easily: a Jewish home is like a bed on a cold night. First you warm it, and then it warms you. Haimish. (Jonathan Sacks, Boston *Jewish Advocate*, 8-28-86). The same person said that

> the Torah is alive to the non-verbal language of furnishing a home. . . . It can wear the signs of its identity — the candlesticks, the framed ketubah, the sepia-tinted pictures of grandparents — with a certain unselfconscious pride.
>
> A Jewish home has its smells. . . . One can almost imagine an olfactory Sherlock Holmes, blindfolded, brought into the house on Friday afternoon, sniffing the air and able to say with precision, "a kugel from Kovno, a borsht from Bratslav."
>
> A Jewish home is a place . . . where the kiddush wine -- that perverse mixture of port and cough syrup — still tastes better than the discreetly supervised Chateau Bois de Saint-Jean. Where children share a common language with parents. Where no guest feels that his footprints are an affront. Where what is most valuable can't be stolen.
>
> Once a week, in such a home, one can almost feel the Divine Presence, welcomed in, made to feel part of the family.

We must remember that the flame of the Jewish family is very fragile. One moment it brings warmth, beauty and light into our homes and our lives, and the next, it is gone. All it takes is a brief moment of neglect, or a cold blast of indifference, to extinguish that beautiful light of the flame of the Jewish family. At this crucial moment in Jewish history, when assimilation is rampant, the flame of the Jewish family is in our hands. It is ours to nurture, protect and preserve. We must keep it burning brightly!

6) Sixth, the Shabbat helps to redeem *society*.

A gentile reporter, after her first visit to Israel, observed in a popular magazine that:

> the official beginning of the Sabbath is at sunset the previous evening, and a notice in the paper tells exactly what time it is. After you've been through a

few of them you can see why. They don't just close the stores; they shut down the whole city. Now that I'm used to it, I'm all for it and think if they'd shut down the whole world one day a week, we wouldn't be in the mess we're in. (*Vogue*, July, 1969, p. 11).

In our society, our lives are crazed, our priorities confused, our days are rushed, our fears and anxieties are numerous, our families are broken, our citizens are addicted to alcohol, nicotine and crack, and we live with a staggering fear of crime. I sometimes wonder if we did a survey in Shaker Heights, Beachwood, and Pepper Pike, to count the number of burglar alarms installed on the doors of homes, and mezuzot on the doorposts, which would be more numerous?

In Gibbon's *Rise and Fall of the Roman Empire*, the author states that it wasn't the invading hordes from outside the borders of Rome who destroyed the Empire, but rather internal decay in the perversion of society's values, which brought its downfall from within. Of all the rituals and values which guarded us, none did so more forcefully than the Shabbat. The Jewish home and the Sabbath have always been a fortress to defend us from the perverted values of the outside world. When we gave up the Shabbat, we broke down those walls, and our people has caught up with our neighbors in juvenile delinquency, white collar crime, divorce, alcoholism, and drug abuse. We used to be immune to these societal diseases, but we aren't any more!

If we look at the rate of intermarriage that is constantly rising in modern society, that too was stemmed by our observance of Shabbat, because it created beautiful memories in the heart of our children which served them well in choosing a mate who would share those memories, and the values they represent. Often in the 25 years of my rabbinate, parents have brought their young sons into my study, and pleaded with me: "Rabbi, tell him not to marry that non-Jewish girl he's going with." After a few minutes of conversation, the young man would inevitably turn to his parents (and friends, if it happened once, it happened 100 times in my own experience), and he would say to his parents:

"Why now? Why all of a sudden do you care about my bringing home a Jewish girl? Why was it OK all of my growing up years to go shopping on Saturday, eat *trayf*, and never make kiddush or light Shabbat candles, and promise me I could quit Hebrew School the day after my Bar Mitzvah, and now — with a sudden outpouring of passionate religiosity, you want me to become the pious Jew that you never were, and bring home a Jewish girl. For what reason should I do that? What heritage did you give me, that I must preserve it by raising Jewish grandchildren for you?"

The sequel to the story is that usually the young woman marries the young man, converts and becomes a better Jew than her father-in-law ever was, and his xenophobic parochialism, masked by a false religiosity, is exposed.

7) **Finally, Shabbat brings to our lives a spiritual feeling that cannot be duplicated in the outside world.**
The presence of the Shabbat bride in our home Friday evening, our attendance at worship Shabbat morning, and the ushering out of Shabbat with a moving *havdalah* service — these weekly Jewish experiences create a spiritual fortress, a Sanctuary in time, that our children crave today. If they do not find this fortress in their religion, they run to drugs, cults, and purposeless lives, drifting aimlessly from one idolatry to the next, with no roots, no home, no values, no direction, no spiritual moorings, and, ultimately, no Jewishness.

The great gift that we Jews gave to the world in creating a Sabbath day, the only holiday mentioned in our Ten Commandments, is one that in some ways we have given away. The Shabbat is an antidote to the boredom, bitterness, stress, anxiety, and the depression that plague many of our lives.

A cartoon in the New Yorker some time ago pictured 2 yogis sitting in a cave on top of a high mountain. Suddenly their serene, quiet meditation was interrupted by the buzzing of a 747 airplane flying by. One yogi turns to the other and he says: "Ah, they have the know-*how* but do they have the know-*why*?"

On Yom Kippur we must ask ourselves, "Do we know **why**?"

Do we know why we have drifted away from our roots and our heritage? Do we know why we are losing our children to secularism, workaholism, drugs, and the god of materialistic hedonism? We must ask ourselves these hard questions and return to truer values.

If we indeed care about remaining Jews, and about whether or not our grandchildren will remain Jewish in the richest sense of that word, then we have to go back to bringing the Shabbat into our homes. We must also bring ourselves to the synagogue for spiritual refreshment and intellectual nourishment. Even more importantly we need to come for a set of values and goals, for *menschlichkeit* and concern for *tikkun olam*: making the world over in the vision of the Hebrew prophets who dreamed of a world of peace — peace in our hearts, our homes, and between nations.

Shabbat At Our Synagogue

The Chinese count their calendar by the Year of the Horse, the Year of the Monkey, the Year of the Dragon. To the Chinese this is the year of the Snake. Let this year for us be : "The Year of Shabbat."

Last year on Yom Kippur I spoke of the pervasive loneliness in our society, and the desire to become more Jewish. We started a program of small, family-oriented groups of our members gather in Havurot once a month for Jewish fellowship. Just one year later 15 Havurah groups thrive in our congregation. They have added an extraordinary dimension of activity, closeness, involvement, and a true *mishpocha* feeling.

It is my fervent prayer, that one year from today, I shall be able to report to you that Shabbat has become a vital force in our synagogue, just as our Havurah groups have become. I pray that Shabbat will come alive and once again be the fortress that preserves and protects us, and enhances our lives with better physical, emotional and spiritual health, more closely knit families who share a Shabbat meal together each Friday evening, and finally, families who feel a stronger affinity to our Creator and the wondrous universe God built for us.

It is truer today than it has ever been before: More than the Jewish people has kept Shabbat, the Shabbat has kept the Jewish People. And may it keep us today — as Jews and as contented, compassionate, and caring human beings.

MYTH

A perceptive person, Muriel Rukeyser, once stated that "The Universe is made of stories, not atoms." Stories are the essence of Jewish history, ethics, theology. Hasidic philosophy is based on stories, as is the Bible, midrash, and aggada (Jewish legends). The Pesach Haggadah, which we read during the Seder, is essentially a story.

> A great story has the capacity to transcend the boundaries of our personal worlds, with their sorrows and joys, and introduce the universality of human experience. Through stories we learn that heartbreak and joy, grief and love, sacrifice and courage are not the territory of any time, any culture, nor are they the blessing or curse of any one individual. Stories remind us how timeless and universal is the search to find peace and freedom, to live with love and courage, and to be free from conflict and pain.
>
> Our imagination is touched by the stories of fairy tales and mythology and of great people who have changed the world around them through the power of their own wisdom and love. We are inspired by the stories of spiritual leaders who teach a path of peace in the midst of hatred and violence. We are equally moved by the story of a child who learns to meet a life-threatening illness with grace or by the story of an impoverished refugee who has found forgiveness for the oppressor.
>
> As we are touched by these stories, we travel in our imagination beyond the limits of our individual experience. Our hearts are opened to feel the sorrow and the courage of another person, to experience the world through the eyes of another, and to empathize with their struggle. As our eyes and hearts open, we begin to see more clearly our own story reflected in the stories of others.
>
> A priceless message of such timeless stories lies in their capacity to move us to look anew at our own lives and our own stories. Great stories teach us not to despair, not to be swamped by sorrow or hopelessness; they remind us in clear and inspiring ways of our own possibilities and potential. The stories of others serve as examples and guides for us, teaching us that the possibility of great courage, love, and compassion can be part of our own story." (*Stories of the Spirit, Stories of the Heart*, ed. Christina Feldman and Jack Kornfield, p. 7)

What is a Story/Myth?

The Exodus story is surely one of the great stories of all human history. It is a paradigm of liberation, just as the myth of Holy Grail is the paradigm of the search for salvation in Christianity. Joseph Campbell, who popularized the power of myth, or the enormous spiritual strength which religious stories convey to their readers and listeners through his many books, tells us that there is really only one story, essentially — that all stories boil down to the same frame or outline. There is a hero, whom Campbell calls "The Hero with a Thousand Faces," because in each culture he has a different name or garb or mission, but he is essentially the same hero.

In the Exodus story, his name is Moses, Moshe. The generic heroes of all stories (like Moses), come from humble birth and rise to a supernatural region of awe and wonder (in our story, Pharaoh's Palace, then his encounter with God at the burning bush). The "hero with a thousand faces" then encounters fabulous forces (Pharaoh's resistance) and defends himself with a decisive victory (the ten plagues, the crossing of the Reed Sea). In the process he bestows great gifts on his fellow humans (the escape from Egypt and receiving the Torah and the encounter with God, establishing the mission of the People of Israel).

Joseph Campbell taught that the grand myths of history are clues to our deepest spiritual potential. "Myths," he wrote, "are stories of our search through the ages for truth, for meaning, for significance. . . . We need for life to signify, to touch the eternal, to understand the mysterious, to find out who we are" (*The Power of Myth*, p. 5).

Let's examine some stories and see if we can learn something from them, as we learn the Exodus story in the traditional Haggadah.

Sample Stories

One way stories convey their power is through a subconscious or sometimes an unconscious message. Here is one that has a clear, but unconscious message:

> Two families had a dispute in eighteenth century Poland. It seems that a member of one of the families was accused of damaging some property of the other family and the issue was creating a great disturbance among all of them. The two fathers argued; the mothers shouted at one another, the many children fought with each other, and the situation was getting out of hand. Neither side would give in, and there seemed to be no solution possible. Finally, the two heads of family agreed that they would take their dispute to the local Hasid, who was a wise and pious rabbi, regarded as the holy man of the area; and they would ask him to render judgment.
>
> Accordingly, the two men requested an audience with the rabbi, and at the appointed time came before him with all their retinue of wives and children. The rabbi asked their problem and they answered him, each proclaiming his own righteousness. The rabbi then asked the men each to tell his own story at whatever length he required. Each of them spoke in detail while the rabbi listened intently, his eyes closed. Finally, when the two men had finished, the rabbi himself began to speak, and all the members of the two families gave him their rapt attention as they listened for his verdict.
>
> He began by telling them how interesting he had found their stories. While he was listening to them, he said, he could not help thinking also of the situation of the Children of Israel when they were in bondage in the land of Egypt.

They also had many arguments there, not only with Pharaoh and their Egyptian taskmasters, but arguments among themselves as well. He was reminded of this particularly, he said, because the time of year was nigh when they would be called upon to remember and celebrate the events in Egypt. He could not help thinking, as they were talking, of the holy days of the Passover season soon to come.

The rabbi then went on to describe to them the thoughts that had come to his mind while each had been stating his case. He had thought of Moses as an infant alone in the rushes of the Nile with his sister Miriam anxiously watching him from the shore. He had thought of the mircle that had made a place for the slave-born baby in the house of Pharaoh's daughter and of the blessing that had followed hm when he had left Egypt in exile. He had thought of the burning bush and the word of God calling Moses, the miracles in Egypt, the deliverance, the struggles, the wanderings in the wilderness, the promised land, and the prophecies which they were now fulfilling in their dispersion among the peoples of the earth.

When the rabbi had finished talking, the two families said 'Amen,' which is a way of saying 'Yes' with religious feeling. They thanked him for having spoken to them and for having solved their difficulty with such sagacity. All the members of the families then shook hands with one another, blessed each other, wished each other health, long life, and a fortunate year. Then they departed, well content with the wondrous wisdom by which their dispute had been settled.

(*The Dynamics of Hope*, by Ira Progoff, pp. 237-8)

What happened here? Simply put, the rabbi transferred the frame of reference from the small world of self-righteous egos to the large universe of sacred time. He shifted the context from the level of two simple families in a small town feeling the pressures of finding security, status, and property, to a different dimension of awareness, a level on which their personal conflict would melt away in their own eyes as inconsequential, because their focus was immersed into the history of the Jewish people as a whole. Our petty conflicts of daily life disappear when we are swept up into the biblical history in which God the Redeemer brings us out of oppression and slavery (which God does in every century). We who have lived through one of the greatest eras of redemption and Exodus from Russia and Ethiopia to the Land of our Ancestors, Eretz Yisrael, know the meaning of the cosmic scale of conflict as opposed to the daily humdrum fights that every family has with some regularity.

In our example story above, on a subconscious level a myth of grand scale solved a personal problem of two families quarrelling over a piece of land. The smaller conflict was submerged into a larger context, the lesson was brought home, and the conflict disappeared. Perspective has been gained.

The following credible, miraculous story, about the Six Day War, like the Exodus story, tells of redemption, salvation, and divine victory over human frailty. Rabbi Hillel Silverman related this story, "Stranger Than Fiction" (UJA, *Orchard*, Sept. 1988).

> When the Old and New Cities of Jerusalem were reunited in 1967, a recently widowed Arab woman, who had been living in Old Jerusalem since 1948, wanted to see once more the house in which she formerly lived. Now that the city was one, she searched for and found her old home. She knocked on the door of the apartment, and a Jewish widow came to the door and greeted her. The Arab woman explained that she had lived there until 1948 and wanted to look around. She was invited in and offered coffee. The Arab woman said, "When I lived here, I hid some valuables. If they are still here, I will share them with you half and half."
>
> The Jewish woman refused. "If they belonged to you and are still here, they are yours." After much discussion back and forth, they entered the bathroom, loosened the floor planks, and found a hoard of gold coins. The Jewish woman said, "I shall ask the government to let you keep them." She did and permission was granted.
>
> The two widows visited each other again and again, and one day the Arab woman told her, "You know, in the 1948 fighting here, my husband and I were so frightened that we ran away to escape. We grabbed our belongings, took the children, and each fled separately. We had a three-month-old son. I thought my husband had taken him, and he thought I had. Imagine our grief when we were reunited in Old Jerusalem to find that neither of us had taken the child."
>
> The Jewish woman turned pale, and asked the exact date. The Arab woman named the date and the hour, and the Jewish widow told her: "My husband was one of the Israeli troops that entered Jerusalem. He came into this house and found a baby on the floor. He asked if he could keep the house and the baby. Permission was granted."
>
> At that moment, a twenty-year-old Israeli soldier in uniform walked into the room, and the Jewish woman broke down in tears. "This is your son," she cried.
>
> This is one of those incredible tales we hear. And the aftermath? The two women liked each other so much that the Jewish widow asked the Arab mother:
>
> "Look, we are both widows living alone. Our children are grown up. This house has brought you luck. You have found your son, or our son. Why don't we live together?" And they do.

The third story tells of the modern exodus from Russia. (*Orchard*, Spring, 1992, told by Rabbi Ed Farber).

> A recent Russian emigrant to Israel learned of the existence of a Holocaust memorial called 'Yad Vashem.' One of Yad Vashem's sacred tasks is the recording of the names of those who died in the Holocaust. So the new emigrant went to Yad Vashem to enroll the names of his family members who were killed in the concentration camps. The man in charge of the records recognized the name of the man's father and mother and told him that these names were registered by another man just a few weeks ago. They checked the records and found the name and address of the man who had listed these names. The Russian emigrant went to the address and rang the bell. The door opened. Immediately the emigrant realized that he was staring at the face of the brother he thought had been killed by the Nazis. Each of the brothers believed that the other had died. Now they had found each other — in Jerusalem.

Telling Stories Hastens Redemption

The last two stories are stories of salvation and redemption, like the original Exodus story. All three stories are one story, as all stories are one story. They tell of God's goodness, of the unity of all of God's creatures, and of God's great powers of redemption. They give us hope that the world in which we labor will yet be redeemed, that Arab and Israeli, Christian and Jew, black and white, Asian, African and American, will one day live in peace, and that God the Redeemer still lives, and will exercise the Omnipotent strong hand and outstretched arm to once again bring us out of the tyranny of repression and violence.

As we re-tell the Exodus story, let's tell a few of our own stories, because stories have such enormous power. Each of us has so many wonderful stories to tell — the same story, and the same theme. We tell of the heroism of daily life, and the resolution of all conflicts that will occur when the Messiah arrives, and the Pesach of the future occurs — when the lion will lie down with the lamb, and nation will not lift up sword against nation.

Robert Fulghum, Unitarian Minister and best-selling author of *All I Really Needed to Know I Learned in Kindergarten*, cites what he calls a "Storyteller's Creed":

> I believe that imagination is stronger than knowledge.
> That myth is more potent than history.
> That dreams are more powerful than facts.
> That hope always triumphs over experience.
> That laughter is the only cure for grief.
> And I believe that love is stronger than death.

It says a lot about stories, doesn't it, this beautiful creed?

I close with a short Hasidic story retold by Elie Wiesel, one of the 20th century's greatest story tellers:

> When the Baal Shem Tov saw difficulty threatening the Jewish People, he would go to a certain place in the forest to meditate. There he would light a fire, and recite a certain prayer, and the miracle would be accomplished and the tragedy averted.
>
> When the Baal Shem Tov died, in the next generation Rabbi Dov Baer couldn't remember the exact spot in the forest where the Baal Shem Tov went, but he did go into the forest, and he lit a fire, and he recited the prayer, and the tragedy was averted once again.
>
> By the next generation, Rabbi Moshe Leib of Sassov not only didn't know the exact spot in the forest, but he also didn't remember the exact words of the prayer. But he lit a fire, and prayed in his own words, and the misfortune was once again averted.
>
> A generation later, when it was Rabbi Israel of Rizhyn whose fate it was to save his people. By that time he no longer remembered any of the instructions of his ancestors. So he sat in his armchair, with his head in his hands, and he spoke to God, saying, "Dear God, I don't know the special place in the forest, I cannot light the fire, and I don't remember the prayer. All I can do, really, is to tell the story, and I hope that this will be sufficient." It was.

When we celebrate memory and tradition through sacred stories, that too helps to bring redemption. As each generation passes down tales from the past, including stories of its own history, we help preserve our heritage and our values. Sometimes, just by remembering the story, it is enough to bring redemption. Let the Seder in each of our homes, as we tell our stories to each other, help speed the Redemption.

EMPATHY: MESSAGE OF PESACH

The ritual and liturgy of Pesach contain many messages, including the importance of freedom: the inalienable right of all people to a life free from oppression, and liberty for every group, race, religion, and nation.

Another significant message is how to become a caring human being. The language of modern psychology calls this *empathy*. Freedom is one of the results of people with power caring for others even though they may lack power. One way to become empathic is to try to identify, understand, and appreciate the situation of the other person from his/her point of view. That is what the Pesach Seder is all about. Do you remember the passage in the Haggadah: *Bekhol dor va-dor, chayav adam lirot et atzmo ke-eelu hu yatza mi-mitzrayim* (In every generation, each person is obliged to see himself as if s/he went out of Egypt)? Psychologists could not have given a more precise definition of empathy. Don't picture ancient Israelite slaves as if they are some far-off, distant, and removed body of people who lived millennia ago. Picture yourself going out of Egypt. It is *you*. That is empathy, formed through the process of getting into the skin of the another person. With empathy, no oppression or discrimi- nation can occur.

Pesach Customs

Over the centuries, a number of interesting customs have developed in our tradition to enable us to empathize with the Israelite slaves. Some examples:

Eating history: Symbols on the Seder plate help us not only intellectually ponder the issues of human freedom, but, as it were, take this historical episode and eat it — make it part of your very flesh.

- Matza: no time to make leavened bread. Picture yourself running out of Egypt, eating matza and almost get out of breath.
- Maror: which leaves such a bitter taste in your mouth you want to spit it out and at the same time spit on the oppressor for his cruelty. Feel the hatred, the anger! Your face becomes as red as the *chrayn* (horseradish). Off my back, you vile oppressor! I will not countenance my people, made in the image of God, to be treated like objects to be exploited and manipulated. I will not accept your cruelty. No, no, a thousand times no!
- Salt water: tears, pain, sadness of loss of a vital part of me: my freedom. Sadness as I watch my children grow up in slavery, never having known the sweet taste of freedom. The sadness in the eyes of my aging parents who anguish over the pain of their enslaved children and grandchildren, their inability to search for happiness, to sing, dance, or celebrate. My pain, my tears, are all too much to bear! So we affluent, comfortable suburban American Jews put a dab of salt water on our tongues to experience a drop of that sadness and pain.

Other customs: In addition to food bringing symbolic reminders of our ancestors, other Seder customs have developed in different parts of the world. Portuguese Jews have a special tradition all their own. They take a piece of the afikoman matza and toss it over their shoulder, pretending to be a refugee from Egypt. This is to experience the haste and the desperation of a fugitive slave. Yemenite Jews pour buckets of water on the kitchen floor, and when they came to the passage I quoted before, all the members of the family walk through the water and feel as if they were going through the Reed Sea. Another common Peach custom is sitting in a leaning manner, like the ancient Romans did in their luxury and freedom, reminding us that our enslavement is ended.

All of these rituals and readings were designed to help us identify and experience, not just *read* about, the condition of slavery. It's not distant, intellectual analysis! The <u>rasha</u>, the wicked son, asks "What did God do for *you*?" (not "for *us*"). He is wicked because he refuses to empathize.

Empathy in our Culture: Four Examples

Several examples in our culture parallel the Seder experience, in which one practices empathy by standing in another's shoes. First, in journalism, modern authors have written stories in which either they themselves or their characters did more than research a life or lifestyle, but temporarily lived it. Choosing to experience life as a black man, the white author John Howard Griffin experiences the difficulties of being black in a bigoted society in the well-known *Black Like Me*. A college president from Haverford College outside of Philadelphia, wrote *Blue Collar Journal*, about an economist who takes a sabbatical. Instead of doing research in some esoteric library, he poses as a garbage collector for three months, then wrote this book about what it's like to be a blue collar worker.

Second, in the field of psychology, Person-Centered therapy, developed by Carl R. Rogers, is one of the most compassionate schools of therapy. One of the leading psychologists of the 20th century and renowned for his books such as *On Becoming a Person*, Rogers died in 1987 in his 80's. He was trained to approach patients in a scientific manner: take a psychological history, analyze the data, and make a diagnosis. (How can one treat an illness/problem without a diagnosis? Any physician, dentist, or psychologist knows that!) But this conventional method was not helping his patients, so Rogers decided to just listen. As he listened, he began to care about the patient and reflect what he heard. He did not analyze or diagnose, but just shared the pain, sadness, and hopelessness. This method lead to the development of Person-Centered therapy, a major influential new school of psychotherapy emphasizing that the most important ingredient in a therapist's work is not academic competence, diagnosis, or intellectual ability, but the ability to get into the other person's neshama and empathize with their personal situation.

Third, in the field of rights for the handicapped, the Gallaudet University story reveals the need for empathic leadership. In Washington, D.C., Gallaudet University, the nation's only liberal arts college for the deaf, appointed a new president, Dr. Elizabeth Ann Zinser, formerly vice president at the University of North Carolina. She is not deaf, and cannot even read sign language. Apparently the quality of empathy, through experiencing the world of the deaf, was not an important consideration in this selection. After strong student protest marches, Dr. Zinser resigned, and King Jordan, a hearing-impaired person, was appointed as the new president. It's amazing that in the 1980's the 21 million deaf and hearing-impaired Americans are still fighting for their rights. Though today there is still much discrimination in employment, wages, and public access, we have certainly made much progress. The empathy lessons of the Gallaudet experience will certainly push the movement forward in helping the deaf achieve their full rights.

Lastly, Elie Wiesel, one from whom we could expect a great deal of compassion for oppressed people, exhibited empathy when he was scheduled to speak at Northern Michigan University. He found out that the lectures were being underwritten by a conservative Michigan publisher, accused of being an agent of the South African government, and cancelled the lectures. When told that 2,500 people would have heard him lecture and were terribly disappointed, Wiesel replied,

> I feel profoundly hurt that I will disappoint some people. But what did I really learn from my life? When it comes to mass humiliation, a compromise is already playing the other side's game. And what is apartheid but collective humiliation; furthermore, it is legal humiliation. In South Africa, humiliation is the law of the land. Therefore, we cannot make any compromise.

How to Learn to Care

Our culture has a low degree of empathy and I find that very sad. There are many ways in which people develop empathy, and for us, it seems, many of these are missing. Rabbi Robert Gordis once said that those who have never suffered are very often insufferable. Suffering and illness and loss somehow are a significant crucible in which character is forged. Fortunately, though, not for all of us. How can those of us who are more fortunate learn to be sensitive, compassionate, and caring, and identify with those who suffer?

One way is to suffer oneself because of a childhood trauma, accident, or loss of a loved one. Personal illness is another means by which people can learn to sympathize with others. Fortunately, most of us miss these terrible experiences. Because of the advancement of medical science, we do not suffer as much from childhood illness, as our forebears did.

Another way many learn the skills of empathy is to care for younger siblings. In Europe, Asia, Africa, children as young as 7 often must take serious, regular care of one or more younger siblings. Studies show that in such widely different societies as rural Mexico, India, the Philippines, and Kenya, child caretakers receive a considerable amount of on-the-job training from adults, who prepare the young children for roles as nurturers. With only one or two siblings, usually, in our society, we often don't learn those skills (*Psychology Today*, Jan. '88, p. 45).

In the field of education, creative teachers have developed ways to inculcate the quality of empathy into their students, making it a regular part of the curriculum. Since the seventies, well-known as the "Me Decade," we seem to have lost the quality which the Pesach Seder tries to carefully to ingrain into our character. We need to recapture it in the educational process. Educational manuals and curriculum guides have been developed which foster the quality of caring and compassion among our young people. For example, in *Learning To Be*, by John Mann (NY: The Free Press, 1972), Mann, an art history teacher, makes this presentation to his students:

> I am showing on the screen a photograph of *Guernica*, a modern painting by the famous artist Pablo Picasso. Now for a moment I am not worried about why Picasso painted this picture, what technique he used, or even whether or not you like it. I only want you to experience more fully what it represents. Suppose that instead of sitting in your chairs you were in the picture. How would you feel? I don't mean that your whole body would be in the picture but that you would sense how the picture feels, what it thinks about. Try that a little bit. Write down what you experience. Then after a minute I am going to ask you to express out loud what you sense in the picture. (A minute elapses.) Now out loud. . . .
>
> "I just want to explode."
>
> "I feel awful, bloody, wounded. This is a terrible place to be, but I can't get out."
>
> "Everything is coming apart. Everything is detached. I will never get back together again."
>
> "Who did this to me?"
>
> "There are guns roaring all around and the smell of burning flesh."
>
> "It is like music — barbaric, loud, horrible music. It keeps getting louder and louder."
>
> [Mann then tells his students,] "Now let these impressions go and I'll tell you something about how and why this picture was created."

This moving Picasso work opens the door for many of Mann's students to feel others' pain, and thus begin to care and connect with them . . . to empathize.

Compassion in Our Lives

The genius of ancient Judaism is that it did not leave to chance the business of growing compassionate people. As a people, we suffered so much that we can feel for others who suffer. In order for that historical memory not to fade, the rabbis created a mechanism to constantly instill the quality of empathy into the adherents of our faith: the Pesach Seder, and many other rituals and liturgies throughout the Jewish calendar.

Rabbi Samuel Dresner defines compassion in a way which sums up our message about empathy:

> Compassion is the pain a father feels when his son hurts his hand playing ball; the pang a mother knows when her daughter is not invited to the party she had her heart set on; the concern a lover has for the least concern of his or her beloved; the anguish which touches a person when someone bears their troubles to them; the tears a child sheds for the limp foot of his dog or the broken arm of her Cabbage Patch; the sigh a judge heaves when he must pronounce a strong sentence; the care a doctor exerts toward a patient in pain; the dull tug at the heart of a soldier when he sees the destruction he has wrought; the help a businessman extends towards a failing competitor; the forgiveness a man grants toward one who has hurt him; the pleading of Moses when the people were to be destroyed because of their golden idol; the weeping of Rachel for the exiles who trudged by her grave on the bloody way to Babylon. It is the eternal mercy of the Lord toward the folly and misery of man.

With the quality of empathy we would all be better people. We would be better husbands and wives, children and parents, grandparents and grandchildren, siblings and friends; if only we could appreciate the fears and hurts of the other. Physicians and health care givers would be better healers if they could appreciate the pain of their patients. Patients would benefit by understanding the endless hours put in by those who heal them. Lawyers would better serve their clients if they could put themselves in the place of an anguished litigant, and clients would more patient with their attorneys if they realized the unending demands placed on their time.

Yes, perhaps Americans and Russians, Arabs and Israelis, could soon end their differences if they could more fully comprehend the longings and dreams and frustrations of the other side. As the poet Longfellow wrote, "If we could read the secret history of our enemies, we should find in each man's life sorrow and suffering enough to disarm all hostility."

If only more people could experience a Pesach Seder, and go through the experience of oppression, and the importance of developing a heritage of caring and compassion and empathy, our world would then be filled with justice and fairness and love, and empathy, as the waters cover the sea.

ROSH HASHANAH — A SECOND CHANCE

Legend has it that George Bernard Shaw sent his verbal sparring partner, Winston Churchill, two tickets to his latest play, with a note saying, "Here are two tickets to my new play. Bring a friend, if you have one." Churchill replied, "I'm sorry, I can't make the first night, but I will try to make the second night, if there is one!"

When a new play opens, after being staged at least once, a playwright has a chance to correct any poorly constructed scenes, improve dialogue, or add something to one of the acts. In such a case, the playwright has a second chance. He can rewrite his play, or at least parts of it. What Rosh Hashanah is all about is giving us a second chance . . . a second chance to rewrite the script of our life, or at least parts of it.

The Akedah

One of the Torah lessons for these holy days is the story of Avraham's second chance. God commands Avraham to bring his only, beloved son, Isaac, the son of his old age, as a sacrificial offering. We all know the end of the story, yet it is still packed with tense drama as we re-read it each year. Yitzchak is saved from near-death — he is not sacrificed. Avraham thus is given another chance as a parent to Yitzchak, an opportunity that he seizes. Now life cannot simply proceed as usual, and Avraham looks at his son in a new light. He begins to act differently as a parent, and immediately sends his servant, Eliezer, to seek a wife for his son. Avraham is acting under the realization, "I almost lost my kid," so he seizes the opportunity to enhance the quality of his relationship with his own beloved child. The Akedah was a learning experience for Avraham, as he learned to look at his child and at life itself in a new way.

In fact, the whole theme of Rosh Hashanah is that through Teshuvah, repentance, through change and growth, we have a new chance at life. Through what our Tradition calls *Chesbon Ha-Nefesh* (introspection, self-evaluation, heightened consciousness of our faults and failures), we have a new year, a *tabula rasa*, a clean slate. We are forgiven for past errors, and can start all over again. What a remarkable opportunity — to rewrite the script of our lives in the coming year.

My colleague Rabbi Saul Teplitz tells the story of angry reader who stormed into a newspaper office waving the day's paper, asking to see the editor of the obituary column. He showed the editor his name in the obituary listing, saying, "You see, I am very much alive! I demand a retraction!" The editor answered, "I never retract a story. But I'll tell you what I'll do: I'll put you in the birth

---

I would like to express my appreciation to Rabbi Jeremiah Wohlberg for the idea for this sermon, and to Rabbi Stephen Chaim Listfield for some ideas which enriched the sermon.

column and give you a fresh start!"

Let's look as two special opportunities which we have in this New Year, to have a fresh start, a second chance, first as a people, and then as individuals.

The Jewish People's Second Chance

In light of the miraculous events of the past year, it seems that our generation is being given a second chance to insure our people's survival. We missed our opportunity 50 years ago during the Holocaust.

This has truly been an historic year, which political columnist George Will called the most interesting, startling, promising, and consequential year ever. Events have been shaped and molded first and foremost through Glasnost in the Soviet Union. The Iron Curtain has been lifted, the Cold War has ended, and the world will never be the same. The Jewish world will also never be the same. The Jews of the USSR and Eastern Europe are in a situation radically different than that which they have been in for the past decades. New winds of freedom create promising conditions for a part of our people whom we have considered lost and cut off for so long.

In December, 1987, over four busloads of our members travelled to Washington, to participate in the most historic gathering in our nation's capital that our people ever mustered. We marched, we cheered, we listened, we did everything in our power to bring Mr. Gorbachev a strong message: **LET OUR PEOPLE GO!** Also, almost two years ago exactly, a Federation mission which Maxine and I had the privilege of helping to lead, brought a group of 40 Cleveland Jews, including 20 form our own congregation, to Moscow, Leningrad, and Kiev. The devoted efforts of Cleveland Jewry in these two great events, together with Jews from all over North America, have finally come to fruition. While during the past two decade many Jews were able to get out of Russia and go to America and Israel, many others either could not get out, or chose to stay.

Today, things are dramatically different. All Soviet Jews fear for their lives because of the terrible rise of popular anti-Semitism. The Chief Rabbi of Israel has issued a halachic decision permitting Soviet Jews to fly from Russia to Israel on Shabbat, because their very lives are at stake. This year alone (1990), so far almost 90,000 Jews have come to Israel. These Jews are not making the same mistakes that the Jews of Germany and Eastern Europe made in the 1930's. Then, too, the handwriting was on the wall, but neither we nor they took it all seriously enough. In a book about that period, *Were We Our Brothers' Keepers?*, Rabbi Haskell Lookstein shows how we let ourselves be fooled by FDR, how we sat quietly and were afraid to rock the boat with our own government, and how our passivity was a factor in the loss of so many Jewish lives.

Today we know differently. We know the power of the Jewish lobby. We know how to march, demonstrate, and organize, how to give of our resources, how to wield influence in high places. And the Jews of the USSR know that unless they get to Israel in time, it may be too late once again. My friends, we have been given another chance! This time we have no excuses. We know the challenge that lies before us. According to Simcha Dinitz, the newly-revised estimate of Soviet Jews who will come to Israel in the next 5 years could be as high as two million, or a 45% increase in Israel's population! We couldn't (or didn't) save 6 million, but now we have another chance — to save 2 million Jews who have been cut off from our people since 1917. We can bring them to Israel, help them learn Hebrew songs, rituals, and prayers, and give them a renewed pride in their heritage, identity, and history.

It is not often in the annals of humankind that we are given another chance. But just as Avraham had another chance at the Akedah, and just as Rosh Hashanah gives us each in our own lives a second chance to start again, we can give our people a second chance to begin their Jewish lives from scratch, and rejoin the worldwide Jewish family as loyal, participating, proud members of the oldest monotheistic religion known to humanity.

We can almost hear God's voice shouting down to us from heaven: "Your generation criticizes actions taken during the '30's and '40's. Here is a test for you, as I tested father Abraham centuries ago. Here is your second chance to redress some of the most egregious errors of the past. We can't change the past, but we don't have to repeat it either!" God might also ask us bluntly, "Are you up to the challenge?"

Thank God there is one place on this planet where a Jew knows that others care about him/her. As thousands enter Israel, Israeli citizens welcome them with open arms. To them it means not only that Jews are being freed from anti-Semitism, it also means that the cost of housing is rising astronomically; that their taxes are going up; new immigrants will fight for their jobs; that tent cities are going up. Yet, despite all that, and despite the grumblings, the people of Israel are welcoming the Soviet immigrants as their brothers and sisters.

A recent news story reports:

> Thousand of Israelis enthusiastically responded to a recent army radio call-in show, and invited over 18,000 new immigrants into their homes, as guests of an Israeli family. Even Menahem Begin, the reclusive former Prime Minister, went on the air to tell the listeners in Moscow, "We are waiting for you."

Begin's words cry out as the voice of the Jewish people: "We are waiting for you!" Fifty years ago millions of Jews could have been saved if there had only been some place or some person on this earth which would have said, "We are waiting for you! You now have a second chance!"

A Second Chance in Our Personal Lives

We as individuals also receive that second chance from God. The Torah reading of the Akedah tells us that Isaac was spared from going under the knife. How many of us sitting here today also were spared the knife, or went under the surgeon's knife and lived to tell about it and thank God for being spared? For how many of us or for someone in our families was there some personal illness, or surgery, which we lived to tell about through chance, fate, or the skill of a surgeon or physician? All of us are candidates for such grave experiences, and none of us knows when it will be our turn. *Mee yichye, u-mee yamut*?

As pastor to my flock, I hear what people say when they escape serious illness, or recuperate, or emerge from danger in one way or another. I never once heard a congregant say to me, "Rabbi, if only I had worked harder in my business!" Never once did I hear anyone say to me, "Rabbi, if only I hadn't spent so much time at home with my spouse or children." But I did hear, and more than once:

"If only I hadn't spent so much time working."
"If only I had run around less, and spent more time with my family."
"If only I had spent less on frivolous luxuries, and given more to charity."
"If only I had been angry and mean less, and showed more patience and understanding."

Indeed these things I have heard many, many times.

Like Avraham Avinu we all have another chance now. Another chance to appreciate our loved ones, praise them, and be kind to them. We can stay home on Friday nights and share a Shabbat dinner with them, not rush through the meal but linger over the candles, kiddush, and motzee. To avoid work on Shabbat morning and go to shul with a loved one or a friend. To take the time to join a havurah, and share Jewish life, holidays, and learning experiences with other members of the community.

The New Year brings us a second chance to do all of these things.

An old movie, "Repeat Performance," is the story of a woman who was angry at her philandering husband, and, finally, in a fit of rage, she murders him. Some time later, she goes to a New Year's Eve party, and while everyone else is reveling and having a good time, she is full of guilt and remorse, and wishes she could re-live her past year. Lo and behold, her wish is granted. Curiously enough, the same things happen, and she has another opportunity to kill her husband. This time, however, she holds back. He asks forgiveness, and she is able to forgive him. Perhaps the story is an exaggeration, and we won't get to change the past. But I truly believe that Rosh Hashanah comes once a year to give us a chance to have a "Repeat Performance": to live differently than we have the year before, to re-assess our values, habits, relationships, commitments, ideals, and dreams, and how we are (or are not) realizing them.

The British statesman Disraeli once wrote:

> Often we allow ourselves to be upset by small things we should despise and forget. Perhaps some man we helped has proved ungrateful . . . some woman we believed to be a friend has spoken ill of us . . . some reward we thought we deserved has been denied us. We feel such disappointments so strongly that we can no longer work or sleep. But isn't that absurd? Here we are on this earth, with only a few more decades to live, and we lost many irreplaceable hours brooding over grievances that, in a year's time, will be forgotten by us and by everybody. No, let us devote our life to worthwhile actions and feelings, to great thoughts, real affections, and enduring undertakings. For life is too short to be little.

My friends, Rosh Hashanah is here again. This time we dare not make the same mistakes as we did last time, for the chance may not come again. This time, let us make use of opportunities to be better people, better Jews, and better citizens. Unlike God, we don't have the opportunity to create a world. But we do have an even better and more important one — a second chance, an opportunity to begin again!

In the words of the poet:

> Life is too brief between the budding and the falling leaf
> Between the seed time and the golden sheaf for hate and spite.
> We have no time for malice and for greed.
> Therefore, with love, make beautiful the deed
> Fast speeds the night.

Fast speeds the night!

THE MITZVAH OF SUKKAH IN THE NEW AGE

A neglected mitzvah is coming back into its own as more and more people are building a Sukkah in their back yards. In some congregations a committee travels from house to house to inspect sukkot built by congregants. Sometimes prizes are offered for the most original, best decorated, or most artistic Sukkah. As a child growing up in Philadelphia, I don't remember anyone on my block, which was exclusively Jewish, who built a Sukkah. What a wonderful change for the better!

I am not certain that the reasons people are returning to the mitzvah of the Sukkah is clearly understood (even by those who are returning to it), whether they can articulate their purpose, or whether, in fact, the matter is entirely conscious. The increased popularity of the custom is, I think, due to the powerful meaning underlying the mitzvah of Sukkah, which people feel intuitively, if not totally consciously. The Sukkah expresses an ideal of something which is missing from our lives in this New Age of heightened spiritual consciousness.

I find eight reasons why the Sukkah is so powerful a symbol and has such strong emotional valence for modern Jews. Eight reasons, perhaps, because the Torah dictates eight days of observance (if we include Shmini Atzeret, on which there is no halachic obligation to dwell in the Sukkah).

First, the Sukkah represents that which is **spiritual** in a world that has become heavily focused on the **material**. While the Sukkah is not plush or fancy, it is among the most beautiful places one can find oneself. With its roof open to the heavens, it brings home its message of God's presence, God's loving protectiveness and shelter, and the awe we feel in the outdoors, far more effectively that does the indoor environment. Our homes are bigger, and our cars more powerful than the Sukkah, but neither rivals its spiritual size and power.

Second, the Sukkah is **simple** in a world that is increasingly more **complex**. *Pirke Avot* teaches us: *marbeh nechasim, marbeh d'aga* — as we multiply our possessions, we multiply our aggravation. Wealthy people today often engage full-time mechanics in their palatial housing complexes to be available to fix and maintain their multitudinous gadgets and machines. The educated consumer will not buy anything mechanical or electronic without a long warranty on parts and labor, and perhaps a long-term service contract to go with it. We spend far too much time fixing, maintaining, and updating our fancy equipment in the pretense that our leisure-filled lives just wouldn't be the same without them.

For the Sukkah, we don't have to shop endlessly to select colors, patterns, or matching fabric. Our Creator has endowed our world with all of the beautiful natural colors possible, and Mother Nature has made incomparable color selections for us in breathtaking splashes of dappled autumn leaves which dot the landscape. The Sukkah reminds us that in some things, **simple** is still better than **complex**.

Third, the Sukkah reminds us that **slow** is still important in a world that is increasingly **fast**. We live on the proverbial treadmill with no time to linger. We are happy if our new individually-designed home can be constructed in a year. Yet the Sukkah is fine even if it takes only a few hours to construct. It takes even less time to dismantle.

In the Sukkah, we don't have a microwave to save time in cooking our Yom Tov meal. In fact, we don't have to save time at all. We have time to sit, relax, and unwind. There is no hurry, and we have nowhere to go afterwards, except to sleep. During the rest of the year, faster is better. In the Sukkah, slower is better. The *longer* we stay in the Sukkah, the better. The slower the meal, the more time there is to enjoy its heavenly shelter. The more time to walk, to sing, to stare, to luxuriate in the presence of Almighty God, and of loved ones. No one will yank away our meal, or our peace of mind. Mark Twain once said that when human beings can travel at the speed of 700 miles per hour, they will yearn to travel once again at 7 miles per hour.

In a world that is increasingly too **fast**, the Sukkah reminds us of the power of **slow**.

Fourth, the Sukkah tells us that **small** is still valuable in a world that is **bigger and bigger**. We measure the value of our homes by the number of square feet, or the number of rooms they contain. In a Sukkah we are happy if there is just one room, a table, and few simple chairs. There is plenty of room for that. No more is needed or wanted.

In the Sukkah we cannot run off to watch television, or hid in the den with our Nintendo games, or be apart from the ones we love and who love us. In the Sukkah, smaller is bigger, less is more, and longer is shorter.

Fifth, the Sukkah is **natural** in a world that is more and more **synthetic and artificial**. One of the rules of the *sekhakh* (roof) of the Sukkah is that it must be made of materials that grow out of the ground. A nail, symbol of the beginning of the advance of civilization, is not permitted. In our hi-tech world, everything is made of synthetic plastics, metals, or chemicals. A Sukkah is only kosher if it comes out of the ground, natural, authentic, real, not grafted, mutated, or genetically engineered.

Do you remember the sign for milk which pictured the Borden cow, under which featured the legend: "Purified, enriched, pasteurized, homogenized." The cow seems to be telling us, "I feel so inadequate!" We feel more adequate sometimes when we know that things are natural, and not synthetic or artificial - — our speech, actions, and intentions. In a world that is increasingly full of the phony, the glitzy, the made-for-TV, the Sukkah captures the ideal of the natural, the real, the true.

Sixth, the Sukkah reminds of us our need for **quiet in a** world that is far too **noisy.** In the Sukkah there is no TV, no blaring radio, no VCR, no boom box, no headphones destroying our gift of hearing, no commotion of traffic careening by us . . . not even any computer keyboard clattering away. It's not like the weddings where the band is so loud that we can't hear each other talk, or the restaurants where the chattering masses, the clanking dishes, pots, and pans, and jostling food servers prevent us from hearing the joy or the pain which the person across from us wants to share.

In the Sukkah the only sounds are the wind blowing the leaves, the trees swaying, the voice of our family and friends, in song and prayer, sharing loving words. The Sukkah reminds us that the still small voice is still larger, greater, and louder than the strongest state-of-the-art amplifier in the world.

Seventh, the Sukkah helps us realize that it's good to be **private** in world where privacy is increasingly invaded. In the Sukkah the phone does not ring, no mail is delivered (by hand or electronically), there is no fax machine. There isn't even a doorbell. In the Sukkah, no one knows, or much less cares about, our social security number, our area code, our zip code, our account number, our credit limit, our bank balance, our net worth, or our tax bracket. In the Sukkah all that's known is what is important to us: our ideas, our values, our opinions, our likes and dislikes, our hopes, our dreams, our ambitions. Not how thick is our wallet, but how big is our heart. Not our Frequent Flier number, our PIN number, but the number of aunts, uncles, cousins, nieces and nephews, the number of people we love, the number of books we would like to read, the number of people we have helped, the number of children we have taught, the number of lives we have influenced, the number of tears we have shed, and the number of smiles and laughs we have shared.

The Sukkah reminds us that our home is our castle, and that only we — each of us alone — owns the key to the chambers of our innermost soul.

Eighth, the Sukkah reminds us that we are to **honor nature**, in a world where the environment is more and more being raped and pillaged. The Sukkah reminds us that a tree is for beauty, not for wood to make drywall. Fruit is to eat, not to process or sweeten, preserve and bottle, and market on a shelf in a supermarket. Leaves are for shade and shelter, and their shapes, sizes, and colors are more important than the frames on our walls or the window treatments inside our lavish homes. The Sukkah reminds us that green means beauty, not money, power, and fortune.

The Sukkah is a symbol of thanksgiving, of a cornucopia of blessings to be grateful for; a place see God's world in awe, not to exploit it, dirty it, waste it, or destroy it. It's a place that is clean, pure, and healthy, where the ground underneath it is not to flatten, develop, pave, or poison, but just to watch, to enjoy, nurture, and honor. In a world that more and more sees nature as something to use, the Sukkah stands to remind us that the environment is a gift to treasure and preserve.

Is it any wonder, then, that more and more people are building a temporary Sukkah behind their permanent homes? Is it any wonder that the Sukkah is becoming a more and more important and powerful symbol of what is truly important for our future spiritual survival in the New Age,? For many of us, enjoying our Sukkah today is more important than it has ever been in the history of human civilization.

VE-CHAI BAHEM — TO LIVE BY THEM

Leviticus 18:5 states, "You shall keep My laws and My rules, by which one shall live; I am the Lord." — By which one shall live — *ve-chai bahem*. The Talmud continues, "*Velo she-yamut bahem!*" (Yoma 85b). This statement implies that it is not only possible to live by God's laws and rules, but to die by them. What does this mean? How can the Torah, mitzvot, the laws of Judaism, be dangerous enough to poison, to kill?

***Live* by the Rules**
How does the Torah promote living by the rules? Examples abound.

1. On Yom Kippur, if a person is sick, should s/he eat? The Torah says to fast. If you interpret this verse, "to live by them" — ve-chai bahem, you realize, that of course one *must* eat. It is not meant to die by the rules, but to live by them. In other words, the rules, rituals, traditions of Judaism are only valid when they give life, affirm life. When they do opposite, we are to disregard them. Or, whenever we practice Judaism, we should be sure to do it in a life-enhancing way, not in a stifling, smothering, killing way!

2. During the days of persecution under harsh Roman rule, when any observance of Jewish ritual brought immediate death, the Talmudic rabbis declared, "*Ve-chai bahem — velo she-yamut bahem.*" Thus, they permitted self-defense during the Maccabean wars. One must violate Shabbat to protect life and Judaism. What good would it be to die by observing the mitzvot and never keep another mitzvah?

3. Some people think Jewish Law, Halacha, is so sacred, being divinely ordained, that they never break the law, and never are flexible. Religion thus becomes restrictive and oppressive. An extreme case involves the Karaites, who sat in darkness all of Shabbat because the Torah says: You shall kindle no light in all your habitations on the Shabbat. The Pharisees, to which we are heirs, had a more liberal interpretation which stated that candles lit before Shabbat could burn all through the night, to enhance Shabbat. That is truly the purpose of Jewish law & tradition — to enhance, embellish, and enrich; not to restrict life and joy. Many ultra-Orthodox Jews don't understand that. To them, there is only one way: their "Torah-true" way.

   A story relates how a man was thinking about the next life, and asked to see heaven and hell. A guide took him on a tour, starting with heaven. While in the elevator, he pointed out the different floors: "1st floor, Reform Jews; 2nd floor, Conservative Jews; 3rd floor, Reconstructionists; 4th floor, Orthodox; 5th floor, secular Zionists; 7th floor, Lubavitch Chasidim." The man asked, "Who's on the 6th floor?" The guide replied, "Shh, that's where the Satmar Chasidim live. Be quiet! They think they are the only ones here!"

4. Our attention is often drawn to rules on Shabbat. For some it's all confining "don'ts": we can't go here, use this, etc. However, true self-imposed restriction can be life-enhancing. The notion that freedom is a lack of rules is not a Jewish one. Self-discipline is an important way to find meaning and beauty in life. But Shabbat is more than rules. It is family, prayer, singing, study, discussion, community, spiritual exaltation. We come together to celebrate a simcha, to share our love, our hopes, our dreams.

Despite the many Shabbat-oriented prohibitions, one of the great miracles of the modern age, Operation Solomon, the Ethiopian airlift, occurred on Shabbat. On May 24, 1991, the State of Israel had the opportunity to save 16,000 Ethiopian Jews by flying them out in one 24-hour period. That unique window of opportunity happened to fall on Shabbat. Operation Solomon was carried out, and every Ethiopian Jew in sight was whisked to Israel on planes. By Saturday noon all had arrived at Ben Gurion Airport. There was not one moment of hesitation on the part of the usually law-abiding, restrictive Chief Rabbinate, because the rabbis utilized the talmudic interpretation of "*ve-chai bahem.*"

5. This year of observance of 500 years of Gerush Sepharad, the Expulsion of the Jews from the Iberian Peninsula, we're paying much attention to the differences between customs of Ashkenzic and Sephardic Jews.

During the days of the medieval ghetto in Eastern Europe, rabbis in the suffocating Pale of Settlement had nothing to do but pile laws upon laws. These ghetto Jews, living with no breath of fresh air from the outside world, had plenty of time to think up new restrictions. Many intentionally lived in isolated villages and small towns, obscure places such as Mir, Berditchev, and Belz, so that their Talmudic studies and religious practice would not be intruded upon by the outside world.

Sephardic Jews, on the other hand, lived in major European cities and ports where commercial intercourse brought them into contact with people from all nations. Their lifestyle was cosmopolitan. Sephardic Jews lived in such thriving metropolises such as Toledo, Barcelona, and Istanbul. With a myriad of cultural influences, Sephardic Halacha was therefore much more flexible. Some examples include:

- On Pesach, Sephardic Jews forbid the use of the leavened form of 5 grains: wheat, barley, spelt, rye, and oats. French & German rabbis added 5 more because they resemble the others: corn, rice, lentils, millet, and legumes. Sephardim permit egg matzah, Ashkenazim forbid it.

- Regarding Kashrut, Sephardic Jews waited an hour or two after eating meat before eating milk; Ashkenazim waited 6 hours.

- On Purim, Sephardim read the Megillah only in the evening; Ashkenazim read it in the morning too.

Self Protection vs. Self-Enhancement

"*Ve-chai bahem*" teaches us an important lesson regarding anti-Semitism. In the Jewish calendar, Yom HaShoah (Holocaust Memorial Day) precedes Yom Ha'Atzma'ut (Israel Independence Day). One looks to the past (the Holocaust), the other toward the future: Israel. Tied deeply to the past, we Jews must never forget it. But our future lies not with remembering past horrors, but with the rebirth and renewal of our people in its own homeland.

Many Jews today think of nothing but the Shoah, anti-Semitism, and destruction awaiting us at every corner. I'm not naive enough to think we should ignore the Pat Buchanans and David Dukes of our society. But neither am I foolish enough to think that fighting anti-Semitism is the be-all of the Jewish people. In *Chutzpah*, Alan Dershowitz's thesis is that the main agenda of American Jewry is to fight off the goyim who are always lurking at the next dark corner. For me, that's not an agenda that carries a vision that will make me want to be Jewish in the 21st century.

Ve-chai bahem, ve-lo she-yamut bahem. If we are to survive, it will be partly because we are careful about our enemies, but even more importantly because we are concerned about the quality of our spiritual and cultural life. The greatest dangers that confront the Jewish People today are not our enemies but ourselves.

We know in excruciating detail how the Jews of Poland <u>died</u>. But what about how they <u>lived</u>? What about their cultural life, their Shabbat observance, their love of learning, their devotion to their synagogues? Why do we study that so little, and morbidly obsess on the details of their last moments of life?

The real problems today are not the few swastikas painted on synagogues or the nasty remarks made by American politicians. Our most intractable and serious problems are the poor quality of Jewish education, the lack of commitment of American Jewry, the shallowness of our synagogues, the single-mindedness of some of our community leaders whose only concern is fund-raising and not how the money is spent to enhance Jewish culture and Jewish religious life.

Ve-chai bahem! We have to worry much more about our future, and the life-enhancing values we transmit to our children, than we should about the enemy lurking at every corner. Jews will not survive by being anti-anti-Semites, but rather by being philo-Semites. We'll survive because of the life-enhancing quality of our Jewish homes and Jewish educational, cultural, and religious institutions.

Self-protection of restrictive laws in Orthodox fundamentalism, on the one hand, and that of people with the victim complex, on the other hand, both share a strategy of Jewish life that says something like this: "Let's circle the wagons and protect ourselves from the outside world." However, while at times we must exercise self-pro- tection, we also must be careful not to live in an ever-narrowing, ever-darkening world, and think rather in terms of being more expansive, more embracing, and more flexible and open to the positive aspects of modern society.

Let me turn for a moment to our Bar Mitzvah boy and say a few words to you.

It is my deepest prayer that when you are faced with hard decisions in your life — continuing your Jewish education, selecting a life-partner who will share your values and commitments — you will not waver. Because you have learned that Judaism is so fulfilling; that the Jewish family is such an important part of your life; that the values of community service, blotting out hatred, violence, discrimination, poverty, hunger and oppression; and cleaning and repairing our world, are so vital; that you look forward to hearing the sound of the shofar, blessing the lulav and etrog, being at a family Pesach Seder, taking a trip to Israel; these significant Jewish values are so indispensable that it will be impossible for you to even imagine life devoid of a true Jewish dimension.

It is my hope and prayer for you that you will want to remain a Jew, not because some people hate us or want to destroy us and someone like you has to fight for us; or that you must keep alive the memory of those who hated us; but because the positive enriching aspects of Jewish life will so powerfully capture your imagination that Jewishness will be a vibrant part of your life from now and throughout the rest of your life.

My deepest prayer is that your search for an authentic and rich Jewish life, one with meaning and purpose, will motivate you to want to live your Jewishness every day of your life. I hope that your guiding beacon will be to "observe My statutes and My ordinances, which, by performing them, we shall live by them" — "*ve-chai bahem!*"

INGREDIENTS OF A JEWISH CELEBRATION

[Delivered October 19,1991, at the Bar Mitzvah celebration of our sons, Jeremy and Yoni]

What are the ingredients for celebrating a simcha? I have found four.

1. First, a simcha must be a time of sharing and giving.
A bar/bat mitzvah child, a bride or groom, any *baal simcha*, is significantly endowed by God with a treasure of spiritual blessings. They receive a chance to stand before God's Aron Kodesh (Holy Ark), in the face of the sacred Torah scrolls, and proclaim heart-felt words of pledging one's life and dreams to being a part of the Jewish people. They stand before the sacred hand-written, lovingly created parchments containing words passed down from generation to generation, and chant words from the ancient prophets whose moral pronouncements have guided 30 generations of Jews, and countless centuries of Christians & Moslems. All these are enormous blessings and privileges, and extraordinary gifts which a bar/bat mitzvah receives as a child of Israel.

One of the strongest teachings which our tradition demands of us is that he who receives must also give. Let no Jew celebrate a simcha without feeling in his/her heart of hearts that we mortals are mere tenants in God's world; not landlords or owners, just tenants. We are here to help, to serve, to give and to care. We are all givers and receivers.

And so, Yoni & Jeremy, I am so proud that a very important part of this celebration today is the request you have made of all your guests, your friends, relatives, classmates, and the whole congregation, to bring food and clothing for those of our brothers and sisters in this community who have less than we who sit in the warmth and beauty of this lavish Sanctuary.

Elie Wiesel, who has been called the conscience of the Jewish People, said, upon receiving the Nobel Prize, "We know that every moment is a moment of grace; every hour an offering. Not to share them would be to betray them. Our lives no longer belong to us alone. They belong to all those who need us desperately."

2. The second thing that must always accompany a Jewish celebration are words of Torah.
Rabbi Alexander Alan Steinbach once wrote: "The Romans used to pray that their children might become rugged and muscular so that they would become good soldiers. But we Jews pray that our children might grow big and noble in spirit, so that they will become worthy followers of Torah."

In the old country, when a young man became a bar mitzvah, he would demonstrate his proficiency in Torah, Mishnah and Talmud by crafting and delivering a scholarly message — yes, even at age 13. By the age of bar mitzvah a young man would have studied for some 8 or 9 years the words of Chumash, Rashi, some tractates of Mishnah and other holy books.

Today, when Jewish education must compete with clarinet lessons, cheerleading, the basketball team, drama, the newspaper club, the debating society and other very worthy academic and non-academic pursuits, we have lowered our standards of Jewish learning. But at least on the bema, our young men and women explain in their own words some of the major ideas of the Sidrah or Haftarah, as a gesture toward focusing on the meaning of the Scriptural lessons of a particular Shabbat, rather than merely on the words and the melody alone, important as they are.

On whatever level, words of Torah must never be absent when Jews celebrate. Saadya Gaon warned us that we are a people only by virtue of our Torah. Only when we call up for attention the teachings of Moshe Rabbenu, Isaiah, Jeremiah, Amos, Micah, Rav or Shmuel, Hillel, Maimonides, Yosef Karo, Yehudah Halevi, Isaac Luria, the Baal Shem Tov, or Rav Kook, and drink deeply a portion of the accumulated wisdom of the generations, can we secure our personal simcha with the values, history, and the bonds of fierce loyalty that our people has demonstrated for the last 4000 years in our own Land and in the Diaspora. Thus, a simcha is not an isolated event, but is the most recent link in a golden chain that reaches back to Avraham and Sarah and all the way down to Jeremy and Yoni.

In a world that is promising yet frightening, rich yet forbidding, hopeful yet still dangerous, where crime, drugs, poverty, war, hatred, bigotry, corruption, disease, homelessness, poverty and hunger abound, we need to proclaim loudly the encouraging words of today's Haftarah, wherein Isaiah uplifts the downtrodden spirits of his flock:

> God gives strength to the weary,
> fresh vigor to the powerless. . . .
> They who trust in the Lord shall be renewed in strength;
> they shall mount up with wings as eagles;
> they shall run and not grow weary,
> they shall march and not grow faint.

What human soul cannot be uplifted on a dreary day by these eloquent and inspiring visions?

3. The third ingredient of a Jewish celebration is an aliyah.

Aliyah is a rich Hebrew word with several layers of meaning. Literally it means "going up," and most frequently refers to the ascension to the bema for an honor at the Torah. A 13 year-old is called to the Torah for an aliyah for the first time halachically when he reaches the age of mitzvot.

Aliyah, of course, also means settling in the Land of Israel, going up to the hills of Judea to attach one's fate and destiny to the re-born people of God, re-establishing their national, cultural, and religious tradition in their ancestral birthplace, Eretz Yisrael.

But Aliyah has one more connotation to the Hebraist: spiritual ascension, rising not just to the bema, and not necessarily to Israel the *place*, but rising morally and ethically, ascending in maturity and sensitivity, climbing higher on the ladder of knowledge, commitment, and understanding, soaring upward in appreciation and awe of God's incredibly beautiful world, in acknowledging and admiring the ineffable sanctity of all living creatures.

Such spiritual ascension must be a part of every Jewish celebration. Rising from our seat to ascend the bema, standing proudly before the open scroll of the Sefer Torah, is a supreme honor which our ancestors recognized as an occasion similar to that of standing at Mt. Sinai with Moshe the very first time the Torah was revealed. So too, is rising to the occasion of becoming a responsible adult Jew an event that contains within it personal meanings that are as important as crossing the Jordan River into one's personal Promised Land, or climbing Jacob's ladder to Heaven and re-affirming the covenant between our people and its Creator.

4. The fourth and last ingredient of a Jewish celebration is simcha — joy.

Simcha is an unusual Yiddish/Hebrew word we use in referring to any Jewish life-cycle milestone. A Jewish celebration must be accompanied and infused with great simcha, great joy. There is joy in knowing that a child is born, or that a young man or woman has reached his or her Jewish majority, or has taken a bride or groom. For us Jews such occasions are events of unparalleled celebration and unbounded ecstasy.

What more important event could take place than knowing that the labors we have expended on perpetuating our heritage all our waking lives are now being affirmed in the most important possible way — by having another generation take up the cudgels for our much-maligned and severely persecuted Heritage. In joy we watch a tender shoot grow a bit straighter and taller by borrowing the courage and vigor of a tradition that has been forged for four millennia on the anvil of trial and ordeal and emerged, even with a limp, yet able to stay in the forefront of the human race for scientific progress, artistic creativity, intellectual prowess, and most important of all, moral rectitude and ethical values.

Such joy is well deserved on a morning like this. When we are able to watch two young men chanting scriptural verses and liturgical passages as easily as tossing a football or sinking a basket. Racing through the <u>Ashray</u> as if it were the latest popular song, and donning their beautifully hand-woven Israeli tallitot as comfortably as they do a double-breasted suit from the latest suburban fashion center.

What greater source of joy can their be for parents, grandparents, aunts, uncles, cousins, beloved friends, and members of the religious community of this congregation? We know that what we believe is being reinforced heartily one more time, with great love and devotion, that our values are being demonstrated yet again by the next generation, and that the historical customs, rituals and principles we live by will remain when we are gone because those who follow us hold them as dearly, if not more dearly, than we do.

What greater joy can there be than resacralizing the words, books, sounds, melodies, cultural conventions, and mores of piety that were transmitted from our great-grandparents to our grandparents, from our grandparents to our fathers and mothers, and now, in this generation, from our fathers and mothers to our daughters, and, in our case, to our sons. Indeed, joy is a pale word to express the pride, the thrill, and the ecstasy a parent experiences on an unforgettable occasion such as this.

So, my good friends, let all Jewish simchas and celebrations contain these four indelible ingredients, and our people shall ever rejoice and be fortified in its ancient faith so lovingly handed down from our ancestors to us, and from us to our descendants:

- The privilege of giving and helping others less fortunate,
- The honor, duty, and wisdom of letting words of Torah suffuse our souls in all aspects of such a celebration,
- The physical and spiritual aliyah that accompany these unique milestones in life's path, so that we can continue to climb and grow in every way,
- And, finally, to give thanks in great joy and song, strengthened by the faith that the song we sing and the dance we dance will be sung and danced by yet another generation after us.

There is, after all, no greater privilege and no greater joy than this in all of God's world.

WHY KASHRUT?

Health and Cleanliness

Maimonides says that Kashrut was established for health reasons. Kashrut shows that even long ago, Jews valued and understood the connection between eating, cleanliness, and health. Examples from tradition include:

1. Eating meat from scavenging animals is prohibited — pigs, etc., are dirty animals.
2. The Schochet examines animals for disease.
3. Before eating, we wash the hands, saying the *b'rachah* ". . . *al netilat yada'im.*"

Modern people ignore the needs of cleanliness, purity, and health. Our air, water, and lakes are dirty; chemicals, pesticides, and antibiotics are used in our food. The Western diet is "polluted" with fats, sugar, salts, cholesterol, and too many calories. Kashrut reminds us to be pure in meeting our physical needs, and that everything we put into our mouths must be "fit" (*kasher*).

Kashrut should include all practices which enhance cleanliness and health of food and the environment, and minimize industrial pollution and waste products. Kashrut should be a reminder to maintain personal physical health standards through regular exercise, careful diet, avoidance of unhealthy substances (tobacco, drugs, alcohol abuse), reduction of stress, adequate sleep, etc.

Jewish organizations, including Federations and synagogues, would do well to be more careful in the meals and refreshments they serve at functions. Too often, menus include things like corned beef, processed lunch meats, eggs, fatty and high calorie desserts. Consider the irony of Jews coming together to discuss implementing Jewish values, and worshipping to improve their own and other's lives, then indulging in unhealthy and unfit (therefore, unkosher) food! When did you last see at such gatherings fruit, salads, and juices instead of the toxic substances we are accustomed to receiving?

Tradition and Jewish Identity

A 4,000 year-old tradition, Kashrut is a distinguishing characteristic of the Jewish people which our ancestors sacrificed themselves to maintain. We should not lightly dismiss something that has been venerated for so long. The weight of proof should rest with those who want to dismiss such strong traditions.

Kashrut kept the Jewish people together as a community — a Jew could eat only at the home of another Jew. Today, a kosher home is more inclusive, because anyone can eat there without worrying. There is no need today to keep us apart from gentiles, but Kashrut is a nice way to keep us close to the community of Israel. Anything that strengthens Jewish identity is helpful in an assimilationist non-Jewish environment.

The practice of Kashrut permeates the home environment, and is a habitual reminder of our Jewish identity, as at least three times a day one must practice the traditions surrounding food. This constant repetition strongly reinforces one's Jewish identity, especially with children who identity is in formation.

For many, the fact that the essential laws of Kashrut come from the Torah, and for some who therefore believe that they are divine in origin, Kashrut thus has extra weight and importance. In the long history of the Jewish legal system, those laws which were "Torah-itic" (*mee-d'orayta*) were more significant, and less changeable, than rabbinic laws.

Self-Discipline

The 1970's and '80's were known for unbridled self-indulgence, the so-called "Me-Decade." Someone said that Americans have no values, just appetites. Our age worships the easy, fast way, having thrown off many disciplines with regard to food, sex, and fun. We lack discipline with regard to:

A. Morals (with extra-marital affairs, bribery, Wall Street scandals, corruption in government).
B. Family (children defy their parents, lack respect for authority, defy their teachers, police, the government; child abuse is a national epidemic).
C. Religion (few want to saddle themselves with the regimen of ritual or the regularity of prayer, holiday, and Shabbat observance; intermarriage rates are up; religious education often comes up last on a list of priorities for children's activities, competing with piano lessons, sports, drama, band and a host of other school functions).

Self-discipline is an important value which Kashrut helps develop. Rising to its challenge affects us in all areas of our lives. We have never needed more than now the benefits of a disciplined life, in an age when any ease or pleasure is the goal.

The Sanctity of Life

Eating acquires a religious nature in Judaism, as one says blessings before and after meals and we wear kippot (head-coverings). In Jewish tradition, the home is the Sanctuary, the table an Altar, the eater a "priest," and the food a sacrifice to God. Eating resembles offering food on the ancient Temple altar through the use of salt on the food (a custom going back to ancient Temple days) and covering knives before reciting grace (Birkat Ha-Mazon). Through eating, we remind ourselves that not just the Temple sanctuary is holy, but the home is also. We need to restore a home with sanctity, when Shabbat, the sukkah, the

Pesach Seder, and the study of Torah have all been taken over by the synagogue. Eating according to the laws of Kashrut restores holiness to the Jewish home, and does not leave that holiness residing only in community institutions.

Humans elevate the practice of eating from the animal level and make it a holy act. To make holy means to sanctify the profane, and hallow the everyday act, especially in the home. The act of eating becomes spiritualized, a religious exercise before the Lord.

Compassion Toward Animals and People

Sanctity of life is also developed through compassion to animals — other living beings created by God. Kashrut insures humane treatment of animals, as we kill the animal humanely and quickly, never hunting or torturing for sport.

Examples of compassionate animal treatment include *Shechitah*, in which ritual slaughter is done by a pious, learned, observant person, not a callous technician. Eating kosher meat, we know that the animal whose flesh we consume did not suffer pain in its death. The Schochet must carefully examine both sides of the knife, lest he use the wrong side and the animal be hurt thereby, run the knife on his fingernails to test for sharpness, and cut the jugular vein to minimize the length of time it takes for the animal to die. The Jew recognizes that blood is a source of life (compare the Biblical expression "to shed blood," meaning "to kill"). Removing blood is tantamount to removing life. Salting and soaking meat, to remove the blood, part of kashering meat, helps the Jew develop an aversion to blood. Even an egg with a blood spot is consider non-kosher.

Kosher laws require a separation of milk and meat, deriving from the well-known Biblical injunction against boiling a kid in its mother's milk. This prohibition makes us understand that animals have feelings just as we do. In addition, animals rest on Shabbat, and the halakha tells us that one's animals must be fed before the master eats. They too are living creatures whose lives are sacred.

Jews avoid killing unless it is necessary to live. Thus, hunting is forbidden in Jewish law, and only a trained, certified schochet can kill animals, and then only for food. In the medieval Haggadah, the "Rasha," the evil son, is portrayed as a hunter. In the Bible, Jacob was the tent dweller, Esau, the hunter. Other examples of avoiding physical cruelty include boxing and bullfighting — decidedly un-Jewish activities which inflict pain on people and animals. *Ever min ha-chai* — ancient practices (before refrigeration) included pulling a limb from an animal and eating it, so the rest of the animal would stay edible. This practice is forbidden by Jewish law as one of the Seven Laws of the Children of Noah (*shevah mitzvot b'nai Noach*), the universal laws of morality applicable to all humanity.

Another Kashrut-related issue is the treatment of people who produce food. Some years ago the Boston *Bet Din (rabbinic court)* declared grapes and lettuce picked by oppressed non-union Mexican Americans to be *trayf* (unkosher). Food produced in an atmosphere of oppression is not kosher. Such a prohibition would also cover the use of flesh or skin from baby seals which had been clubbed.

Kashrut also asks us to be conscious of world hunger. The blessings over food recited before and after meals help us appreciated God's bounty in giving us the food that sustains us. Awareness of less fortunate people is a natural consequence of such an expression of gratitude. Such awareness could lead to concrete acts of charity (*zedakah*), such as making a contribution to the national Jewish organization which alleviates world hunger: MAZON: A Jewish Response to Hunger. *B'rachot* (blessings) over our sumptuous meals can thus lead to sharing our bread with the hungry (cf. Isaiah 58:7 - the Haftarah of Yom Kippur morning).

Conservative Judaism

Kashrut distinguishes Jews from other groups that hold different principles. Pagans in the ancient world, for example, would gorge themselves at eating orgies, then use emetics to disgorge and eat more. There was no limit as to what they would eat: dogs, pets, any animal, crawling or creeping thing. Another different view of eating comes from Christianity, which states in the Gospel according to Paul (in the New Testament), "Only what comes out of a man's mouth makes him pure and impure, not what enters the mouth." This is a clear distinction from Judaism.

Reform Jews generally do not keep kosher due to their principle of autonomy, though today more and more are recognizing Kashrut's importance, and are taking up the practice in varying degrees. Many Conservative Jews, though they may not keep a kosher home, will insist on at least holding kosher weddings and parties for Bar/Bat Mitzvah. At a religious simcha, food including shrimp, scallops, ham, and mixing meat and milk are odious to traditional Jews. Conservative Judaism broke from the Reform Movement over a trayf (non-kosher) banquet on July 12, 1883. This is a watershed date in American Jewish history, at which point the Conservative Movement was born, stating clearly, "Here we stand, this is where we draw the line."

I will leave you with some issues which Conservative Jews struggle with regarding Kashrut: How consistent must we be? Do we practice at home but relax our discipline at restaurants and in others' houses? What is the role of consistency in ritual? Are there levels of Kashrut? Can we see Kashrut as a ladder, or "do as much as you can?" Kashrut with all of its related issues, is a cornerstone of Judaism. I urge you not to take it lightly, and to explore its meanings and implications for you, your families, and the Jewish people.

REFLECTIONS OF AN AMERICAN JEW

America is a pluralistic society, we're told, with no official race, creed, or religion. For me, an American, a Jew, a rabbi, this notion is a grand myth. I have found America so permeated with the trappings of Christianity that I frequently feel like an outsider, a stranger, a member of a tolerated majority. As December 25 approaches, and America garbs itself in red and green, this feeling intensifies.

Our vocabulary has acquired some new additions in recent decades. We have "racism," discrimination against members of one race by those of another. "Sexism" describes the discrimination of members of one sex against those of the other. I propose a new term, "religionism," meaning discrimination practiced by the majority religion in this nation against members of a minority religion.

"Another paranoid Jew?" you might ask. One of those Holocaust-mentality/Masada-complex Jews, who sees a Nazi lurking in every corner? Maybe so. But there is a fine line between fear and paranoia. Paranoia is unjustified fear. Normal fear is useful, protective, necessary, and healthy. I am comfortable being a Jew, and that will never change. The experiences I will describe are real to me. As such, they should be recognized by my Christian neighbors, who must decide whether to ignore or change the situation. The ultimate goal of American society ought to be to improve that society, make it a more just and fair place to live, not merely to make it "easier" for Jews or any other minority.

Thus, I write as an American to other Americans of all faiths who want to share with me the task of "perfecting the world under the Reign of the Almighty" (from Jewish traditional liturgy, the "alenu" prayer).

I live in a country which, upon its creation over 200 years ago, legislated a separation of Church and State. However, the *de facto* association of "American" culture with Christianity strongly continues to this day. The reminders that I am a member of a tolerated minority are ubiquitous. The list is legion; my anger about them is cumulative. Each reminder deepens the hurt of the previous ones, making its effect more lasting and more painful. M i n d you, as an observer, I love seeing beautiful Christmas decorations in December, and am moved by the spiritual depth of my neighbors praying to Jesus, and thoroughly enjoy listening to the beautiful music of the Christian holidays. My objection arises when these events and experiences are assumed to be the sole acceptable cultural/ religious/ethnic property of all good Americans. At this point, my temperature rises and my dignity is affronted. I deny the equation between America and Christianity, and expect my non-Jewish friends and neighbors to respect my right to be simply me: a Jew, non-Christian, a full and loyal American who chooses to be religious and/or spiritual in ways that differ from the doctrines and/or practices of Christianity.

Christian Chronology

A prevalent reminder of the American-Christian culture can be found in textbooks, newspapers, and magazines. Chronology is divided into two periods: B.C., or Before Christ (Messiah and Savior to Christians), and A.D. (Anno Domini), "in the year of our Lord." "Our" Lord, mind you. Gentiles may not know this, but in Jewish books it is customary to refer to time periods as B.C.E. — "Before the Common Era," a euphemism for the birth of Jesus — and C.E., "Common Era." It would be absurd to suggest an entirely new chronology, beginning, perhaps, with the calcolithic age. Or would it? At the very least, I expect not to be required to state that today is October 7, 1995, in the year of "our" (whose?) Lord.

My insult and injury were restored to the conscious level recently when I bought a Seiko watch, which displays the time and day of the week in English and Italian. Since Seiko's largest market is in Italy, I don't mind the option of displaying the days of the week in English or Italian. However, on Sunday, my choice is either SUN or DOM, both illuminated in bright red. Thus, all day on Sunday, I can glance at my watch and see — in that distinguishing red — that this is a special day, the sabbath of my gentile neighbors. Here is another reminder that I live in a culture dominated by Sunday-sabbath, when my own Shabbat begins Friday night and concludes Saturday at sundown. Vestigial Sunday Blue Laws also remind me of the special status of Sunday, (though for the most part, they are ignored or have been repealed). My shiny new watch, however, cannot be repealed; it can only be sold.

Some years ago, I received a letter from the President of the United States, addressed to clergy of all faiths, declaring Sunday (*sic*!), March 26, 1972, as a "National Day of Prayer" for our prisoners of war in Southeast Asia. We were asked to read the President's Declaration of that event in our houses of worship at prayer that day. While we do have prayer daily in synagogues, including Sunday, I assume that the President wanted it read on the Sabbath, when most worshippers attend, not at a daily morning service of minor attendance. Most importantly, the words A.D. were spelled out in English, and I was asked to read this in my synagogue! Namely, that this day, March 26, in the year of "our" Lord, 1972, was a special day of prayer for all (?) Americans.

The "Christian Thing to Do"

As a Jew and a rabbi, I have often received questions about how my house of worship and its practices and customs differ from those of the majority religious group in America. "What does your church think about that, Rabbi?" (I worship in a synagogue, not a church.) "What does the Old Testament say on that issue?" Answer: You refer, of course, to the Hebrew Bible, as opposed to the New Testament. My Bible is not an Old Testament, since it has not been superseded by a *New* Testament, in my faith.

At other occasions, I stand in a gathering for the observance of Thanksgiving, or at a peace rally or some other common American celebration, observance, or civic event, and I am prayed for by a well-meaning priest or minister who blesses me "in the name of the Father, the Son, and the Holy Spirit." Thanks, but no thanks.

I might receive a letter requesting charitable aid, asking me to make a financial contribution to the Community Charity Fund, "in the spirit of Christian Charity." At a local meeting of a community service organization, I am asked to "do the Christian thing" — *e.g.*, be loving, compassionate, etc. A letter reached me recently from the Red Cross, a worthy organization which deserves our support. The letter reminded me "to donate blood, and thereby share my gift of life in the spirit of Christmas."

In public schools, my children are asked to sing Christmas carols (not merely listen to them, something different), and decorate the Christmas tree ("An American symbol, no longer holding religious connotations" — tell that to your local parish priest!).

When I serve as a congregational rabbi, I make weekly visits to several hospitals to see my parishioners (oops — my congregants). One hospital's chaplain's office was kind enough to keep 2 large file boxes on the receptionist's desk with cards for all patients according to their religion and church. One box contained only Catholic names, and the other held the various Protestant denominations. "Hebrews" (a word used in the 19th century for American Jews) were apparently, at least in the eyes of the head chaplain, just another Protestant denomination. My congregation, Beth Yehudim, was filed between the Baptists and the Presbyterians.

Doing My "Jewish Thing"

What do I really want?

I write as one who wishes to live life as a full human being, doing my own (Jewish) thing.

I write in frustration, hurt and anger, but without acrimony. I write with hope and love, not with hate or unmitigated despair. I do not ascribe ill intentions to my neighbors, just ignorance and insensitivity.

I ask that we take a good hard look at "religionism" as one of the major psychological oppressions of 20th century American life.

I write because I love my country, its history, people, traditions, and its democratic spirit. I write because I care enough for Americans to criticize some of them.

The Hasidic master Reb Levi Yitzchak of Berdichev tells of learning the meaning of love from a drunken peasant. While sitting at an inn, he heard two peasants talking next to him. With their cups emptied several times, they were throwing their arms around each other and making effusive expressions of caring. Said Peter to Ivan, "Ivan, what hurts me?" Ivan replied, "Peter, how should I know what hurts you?" Peter replied, "If you do not know what hurts me, how can you say you love me?"

Now, at least, my readers know what hurts me.

IS JUDAISM A VINDICTIVE RELIGION?

If the Scud missile attacks on Israel (in January, 1991), the destruction of houses and loss of life in Tel Aviv, and the dreaded fear of a coming gas attack were not enough, Israel and the Jewish People have to suffer one further indignity — this time not at the hands of Saddam Hussein, but the American media. Is it possible that journalists and news broadcasters are harming the Jewish People today in their coverage of the Gulf War? Yes indeed, they are! They are harming our people and our faith by dredging up one of the oldest and most distorted misconceptions ever perpetrated upon the Jewish religion That Judaism is a religion of vengeance and vindictiveness; that the so-called "Old Testament" God reeks of retribution, severe punishment, and hatred.

Such attacks on Judaism are not, furthermore, the expressions of only the well-known Israel-baiters, such as Pat Buchanan, Evans, or Novak. We are speaking now of many of the mainstream media personalities, popular TV programs and news weeklies.

Let me cite just a few examples from the past week or two. Sunday morning, I listened to NBC's "Sunday Today," which is not exactly known to be extremist, racist, or bigoted in the David Duke mold. In describing Israel's admirable quality of exercising self-restraint since the Gulf War began, the broadcaster reminded his listeners that this unprecedented behavior on the part of Israel is a marked departure from "Old Testament vengeance."

A second example: The January 28 (1991) issue of *Newsweek* manages, in the space of a two-page article, to slip in three insults to Judaism and the Jewish people, not to speak of the State of Israel, in its view the modern reincarnation of "Old Testament vengeance." In an article on the war we are informed that "with grit and spirit, the nation that never turns the other cheek managed to refuse Saddam Hussein's early invitations to transform the gulf conflict into an Arab-Israeli holy war." On the same page, further in the same article, we find a young Israeli teenager, Ronit Israeli (note the name — even it reflects the nation, the state, and their biblical ancestry), who swears that "We will give them back twice what they did to us." Later in the same article we read that Israel has many alternative methods of dealing with Saddam — one of which is that "the Israelis could send the Air Force or their Jericho missiles to hit Baghdad civilian areas in an eye-for-an-eye retaliation."

From where does all of this bad journalistic theology emanate? It is neither the discovery of NBC News nor *Newsweek* magazine. Its history begins, at least in part, in the misinterpretation of a biblical verse from the Book of Exodus, 21:22-25:

> When men fight, and one of them (accidentally) pushes a pregnant woman, and a miscarriage results, but no other damage ensues, the one responsible shall be fined according as the woman's husband may

exact from him, the payment to be based on the judge's determination. But if other damage ensues, the penalty shall be life for life, eye for eye, tooth for tooth, hand for hand, foot for foot, burn for burn, wound for wound, bruise for bruise.

This passage is meaningless unless one understands its legal context and compares it to other ancient Near-Eastern cultures. To the uneducated reader, it sounds harsh and punitive, proclaiming the cruel doctrine of the barbaric ethic of retribution.

Lex Talionis

Vengeance as a character trait has never been looked upon favorably by enlightened humanists. Something more in character with the verse in the biblical Book of Proverbs would be the choice of the person of modern, civilized behavior: "A soft answer turns away wrath" (an "Old Testament" statement, we should note).

However, that is not what this passage from Exodus means. The law of "an eye for an eye" emerges out of a background in which assault and battery were private wrongs, and could be settled between the families of the assailant and the victim. Even in the time of Babylonian King Hammurabi (one of Saddam Hussein's predecessors, since Iraq is now located on the site of ancient Babylonia), several centuries before Mosaic Law, the state began to take jurisdiction over such matters to prevent society from the effects of violence and counterviolence. It even went so far, in some cases, as to assign monetary payment for loss of limb in place of punishment in kind.

When King Hammurabi proclaimed his so-called Lex Talionis, the Law of Repayment, he was following already-established legal tradition in the pre-biblical world, of commanding fair punishment for crimes of assault and battery — only one life for one life, only one eye for one eye, etc. By the time the Torah introduces the Lex Talionis in the Book of Exodus (and in 2 other passages, Lev. 24:17-22 and Deut. 19:18-21), it bore witness to a legal revolution which demanded exact justice equally distributed, not adjusted penalties for different social classes, and not punishment out of proportion to the crime. It was the beginning of dealing with injuries inflicted upon a human being in a way that precluded blood feuds, some lasting for generations, a custom which still prevails in many Arab countries, as well as in contemporary mountain regions in Appalachia. The notion was that the punishment had to fit the crime. An "eye for an eye" meant "*only* an eye for an eye, and not a life for an eye." Furthermore, punishment was to be made by monetary compensation, no longer through actual physical retaliation. Biblical law now implied "the equivalent of an eye for an eye," though the phrase remained unchanged.

Following are the words of Prof. William Foxwell Albright, a Christian minister (d. 1971), widely acknowledged by Jew and Gentile alike as one of the 20th century's leading biblical scholars.

> The original ethical intent of Mosaic law has been badly mangled by misinterpretations of the so-called *lex talionis* -- life for life, eye for eye. This is often considered as vindictive cruelty which survived somehow from the barbaric past. Actually it is the first formal enunciation of the principal of equal justice for all and it put an end to the pre-Mosaic practice of exacting heavier penalties from the lower classes than those of high social ranks. The "eye for eye" meant, in fact, "Let the punishment fit the crime" and had no more to do with revenge than the Hebrew concept of the "Avenging God" has to do with vengeance in the modern sense. In Hebrew avenge meant, "to champion, defend, vindicate" -- as we have determined from cuneiform letters written during the four centuries before Moses.

Pernicious Journalistic Theology

If the "an eye for an eye" passage does not connote base vengeance, and its real meaning is that of bringing a greater sense of justice to society, why do journalists and others continue to perpetuate the perfidious notion that Judaism is a religion of vengeance, wrath, and cruel punishment, and that the State of Israel is merely carrying forward and old and inbred tradition that came from its people's Bible? Furthermore, why do I call it pernicious journalistic theology?

The answer is that this attack on Judaism goes as far back as the New Testament, and it has been continued as an invidious comparison between Judaism and Christianity for the last 20 centuries. Earlier I cited the biblical verse whose misinterpretations is the source of all of this misunderstanding. A verse from the New Testament made the misunderstanding permanent and carved the notion of an "Old Testament" God of wrath and vengeance deeply into the consciousness of Christian civilization.

Turning the Other Cheek?

"You have heard that it has been said, 'An eye for an eye, a tooth for a tooth': But I say unto you, that you shall not resist evil; but whoever shall smite you on your right cheek, turn to him the other also." (Matthew 5:38-39).

The Gospel of Matthew is putting the notion into the mouth of Jesus that he has come to replace the "old" law of Judaism, the "old" covenant, or "testament" of the Torah, with a new covenant, a "New Testament," espousing a more highly evolved and more mature concept of a loving, caring God, who tells his followers this:

> Instead of striking back cruelly at your assailant, stand there and take it! Not only should you stand there an take it, and not hit back, but after he smacks

you on one side, turn your head around and give him the chance to strike you on your other side. How humane, moral, and elevated you will be in God's eyes if you behave in this new way, and reject the old way of "an eye for an eye."

Not only is this an idea different from the Jewish approach, and a bad strategy in Jewish eyes if one wants to stay alive, and not only does it make hard-to-understand theology, but it is a literary and historical lie! The Christian strategy totally distorts the meaning of the biblical concept of "an eye for an eye," as we have seen, and make an odious comparison between Judaism and Christianity. Comparisons are often odious, and, sometimes, as Shakespeare called them, odorous. This one, if you forgive the pun, smells to high Heaven.

Had I more space, I could quote dozens of passages in the Hebrew Bible which point to the importance of love, compassion, mercy, and kindness — concepts permeating our Scripture, as well as post-biblical Hebrew literature. I could also point out just as many verses in the new Testament that reek of anger, wrath, punishment, and retribution. The negative comparison really does not hold water. What is even more distasteful is how some modern Christians continue to perpetuate the myth implied in this insulting comparison, and make the State of Israel, the Jew of the nations of the world, bear the brunt of their supercilious self-righteousness.

The great Russian writer, Tolstoy, wrote in his autobiography, *Confessions*, that he once studied the New Testament verse I quoted above with a local scholarly rabbi. The rabbi turned to Tolstoy and asked him, "Do Christians obey this command of turning the other cheek?" Tolstoy then records the following thoughts: "I had nothing to say in reply, for I realized that in every land means were employed for the punishment of offenders. And, further, at that particular time Christians were not only not turning the other cheek, but were smiting the Jews on both cheeks."

A modern Christian theologian and scholar, James Parkes, adds this further thought to Tolstoy's remarks: "In fact, it is only in some parts of the Christian world, and in the 19th and 20th centuries, that Christian justice has begun to approximate the sensitivity and compassion of Jewish rabbinical courts fifteen hundred years earlier."

Resist and Destroy Evil

The greatest irony, though, is that this whole Persian Gulf War is based not on the Christian doctrine of love and "turning the other cheek," but rather on the proudly Jewish notion that we must resist evil and destroy it in order to bring to earth the Kingdom of God. President Bush and all of the nations who joined him in this grand coalition which is unprecedented in the history of modern diplomacy, have launched an all-out attack on Saddam Hussein and his war machine precisely because to sit back and let Evil reign in the world is one of the greatest sins that any leader or any nation can commit. How fortunate the world is that it is the "Old Testament," or as we say, the biblical notion of justice and fairness, that enabled all of these nations to tell Saddam Hussein that he cannot succeed in raping, robbing, pillaging, and pulverizing a neighboring country with impunity.

The fact is that no people, no religion, has a monopoly on the truth, and we must all work together if we are to create the new world order of which President Bush has spoken. But let it start with a deep and deserved respect for one of the noblest and ancient traditions whose high moral code is the basis for civilized justice for every person, every faith, and every nation involved in this war.

CREDO OF A MODERN JEW

1. A Jew should search for the meaning of God in his/her life. A Jew should take seriously the question: What is God, and how does belief in God, accepting "the yoke of God's kingdom," affect my life?

2. A Jew should make the home the central focus of Jewish commitment. The most important events in human life and Jewish life take place in the home: formation of bonds of intimacy and loyalty, training and education for living, study of Torah, celebration of Shabbat and holy days as well as of life's milestones. Through observance of *mitzvot* such as *mezuzah*, *kashrut*, Shabbat and festivals, the study of Torah, the Jewish heritage is perpetuated first and foremost in the Jewish home.

3. A Jew should identify with the Jewish People, its history, its historic homeland — *Eretz Yisrael*, and the modern State of Israel. A Jew should feel a part of the Jewish People vertically (historically) and horizontally (participating in contemporary Jewry). A Jew should be aware of what is happening in Jewish communities throughout the world. A Jew should associate with other Jews and support Jews in need financially, culturally, and personally — through visits to places like Israel and Russia.

4. A Jew should belong to a synagogue which is, along with the Jewish home, the central institution of Jewish life. The synagogue is the focal point for expressions of Jewish religious, spiritual, cultural, educational, philanthropic, and social life.

5. A Jew should make Shabbat primary in personal and family life. Friday night Shabbat dinner, Shabbat morning in the synagogue, and Shabbat afternoon at home and in the community, all help the Jew find meaning in life, intimacy through family and community, and express the higher purposes for which human beings are created.

6. A Jew should make the mitzvah of *Talmud Torah* (study of Torah, Jewish knowledge) a lifelong pursuit from cradle to grave. Study is the intellectual, cultural, and spiritual basis for all Jewish ethical and ritual living. The perpetuation of the Jewish literary and artistic cultural heritage depends on the continuous immersion of Jews in our past and is the —sustaining life force which gives motivation and direction for the Jewish future. Talmud Torah (study of Torah, Jewish knowledge) is, according to tradition, the highest form of divine worship.

7. A Jew should be and act like a *mensch*. *Menschlichkeit* is the outcome of a way of life filled with *Talmud Torah* and *mitzvot* (good deeds). A Jew should adhere to the highest standards of ethics and morality possible, and should strive to practice in personal, interpersonal, professional, and business life, the highest possible standards of Jewish and human ethics.

REQUIREMENTS OF A CONSERVATIVE JEW

In the story of Abraham's quest for a wife for Isaac, the actions of Abraham's servant Eliezer reflect on the meaning of Conservative Judaism for the 1990's and beyond. Abraham, having just buried Sarah, is aware that his days may also be few. His main concern remains to find a nice Jewish girl for Isaac, his son. Abraham makes Eliezer swear to find such a Jewish woman. How would he recognize her? Rebecca, the woman Eliezer determines is right for Isaac, displays four characteristics which live on for us as ideals to which all Jews can aspire.

1. Loyalty
"*El artzi v'el moladetee taylekh!*" (Gen. 24:4)
First, as the above verse demands, Rebecca is loyal to the motherland. The importance of such loyalty cannot be underestimated today, when the whole world turns its back on Israel. In our isolation, we must stand firm, resolving to fill Israel with more than just planeloads of Christian pilgrims.

We are Zionists because Zion is ours. We love Israel because it is our Homeland. We don't love our parents just because they are perfect or flawless -- we love them because they are our parents, and they gave us the gift of life. Israel can make a mistake now and then. At least in this democracy (the only one in the Middle East), to clear up a public or government scandal, a study is commissioned and errors are admitted, rather than a mysterious series of disappearances or assassinations being carried out.

When I heard that Meir Kahane was assassinated, I was outraged. Yet I had to ask myself why. I oppose his racist viewpoints, his rabble-rousing. Never would I walk across the street to hear what he had to say. Was it because he was a human being, and no one deserved to die by an assassin's bullet? Only in part; that does not account for the degree of anger I had. Then, when I saw the pictures on TV of thousands of Jews crying over his casket and shouting in their anger, I became more angry, and felt, just for a moment, that same desire for revenge felt by his followers. I must admit I was perplexed, and wondered why I was so angry.

Then I read an analysis given by Dr. Samuel C. Heilman, professor of sociology at Queens College. He maintains that the reasons for the huge outpouring of feeling were quite different from what most people thought. After all, Kahane was marginal both in Israel and in the US, and not popular in the Jewish community anywhere except on the radical fringe. Heilman posits, "In his death, Kahane came to represent two things. He was shot in public by an Arab, and nobody wants to say it is open season on Jews. Secondly, the man who shot him was striking a blow at Israel." Now I could understand the passion, the fury I felt at the assassination of even one such as Meir Kahane. It wasn't only his death I was furious about, but what it symbolized: one more blow against our people and our Homeland.

A Conservative Jew is passionately committed to the welfare of Eretz Yisrael and Am Yisrael, to that part of Kahane's teaching that said that Jews can no longer afford to be passive about Jewish survival and the welfare of Zion and Zionism. We have to be tough, loyal, passionate, and fierce in our self-defense. We cannot let Saddam Hussein, Yasir Arafat, or Muamar Kaddafi determine when we can travel to Israel, or if we will feel safe in our own Homeland. Let us emulate the thousands of Soviet Jews pouring into Israel, who are less concerned about Saddam than about their anti-Semitic neighbors in Kiev, Leningrad, and Moscow.

This example leads to the next qualification of a Conservative Jew. We must be fierce and determined in our self-defense, as Kahane was, but not cruel or racist.

2. Kindness

In our Genesis story, Eliezer does not know how to determine which young maiden he should bring home for Isaac. He prays for guidance, and the idea comes to him: When he reaches the town where Abraham came from, he will go to the well. He knows that the young women gathered at the well will greet him, and he will ask them, "Please, lower your jar so that I may drink." One of the maidens will no doubt reply, "Here is water for you, and let me also give water to your camels." This is Eliezer's test of character: the woman who thinks not only of him, but also of his animals, must be kind-hearted, and she will be best one for Isaac!

Rebecca, the chosen maiden, is not only kind, but the Torah calls her "*tovat mar-eh*," a beautiful woman. How does Judaism define the beautiful person? The Torah says nothing about the clothing Rebecca wore, whether stylish or not. We do not learn about her complexion, if her skin is soft or weathered, if she is thin or plump, tall or short. The details of the story relate *how she treats people*. How does Rebecca speak to Eliezer, the servant? She offers hospitality, reaching out to the wandering stranger in her land, unaware of his identity or that he seeks a bride for Abraham's son.

A colleague of mine visited a Conservative shul as a guest speaker. After the service, a man told him that he had just moved to town, and had come to shul that morning before the service began. He stayed to the end and attended the kiddush afterwards. The man related that though he spent over 3 hours in shul, only one person spoke to him, and that was to say, "Hey, you're sitting in my seat!"

The Conservative synagogue must become a more caring community. We must reach out to people, and let them know that we Jews are kind, concerned, warm people of character and compassion.

3. Awareness of God

When Eliezer suggested that Rebecca return with him to meet Isaac and be his wife, her brother and father respond by saying, "*May-adonay yatzah ha-davar!*" ("This matter has been determined by God!") In other words, it's not up to us to decide, it's up to God. My esteemed colleague, Rabbi Rami Shapiro, has written:

> Our Torah is a light,
> > our deeds a lamp.
> It is the task of the Jew to bring light
> > to the dark places of the world.
> Where the world is blackened by the smoke of war
> > the Jew must bring the light of peace.
> Where the world is darkened by illness and suffering,
> > the Jew must bring the light of healing.
> Where the world is bleak with broken hearts,
> > the Jew must bring the light of kindness and caring.
> Where the world is dim with hatred and lies,
> > the Jew must bring the light of love and truth.
> We are the light bearers and Torah carriers.
> We are the doers of mitzvot,
> > those great and simple acts of love
> > that heal our hurting world.

Rabbi Robert Gordis, dean of ideology of Conservative Judaism, titled one of his books, *Leave a Little to God*. He explains the meaning of the title:

> The great Solomon Schechter, the first president of the Jewish Theological Seminary, was accustomed to repeat [this phrase:] "Leave a little to God." Note what he did not say. Not, "Leave it all to God," for then man becomes nothing. Nor, "Leave nothing to God," for then man is doomed to failure. "Leave a little to God" — that is the counsel we need. We must do our share and know that God will do his. *Action and faith both must be our watchwords. To work and to wait must be our program — passion and patience, both are needed for life.*

The Conservative Jew must be aware of God's presence in all things, yet not leave it all to God. One must work together with God to accomplish the *tikkun olam*, the new society based upon justice, equality, and truth. One of the most sacred tasks of the Jew today is to work as God's partner in improving the environment, providing for the poor, fighting aggression, ending corruption, cooperating with nations of good will toward a peaceful and just world.

4. Women's Rights

Finally, when the ultimate decision is made for Rebecca to be sent to Isaac, her family insists that she be consulted: "*Nikrah la-naara, ve-nishal et piha!*" "Let us ask the young woman what she wants." (Gen. 24:57) Consideration is given to Rebecca's wishes.

Conservative Jews have realized that modern women have full and equal rights in our movement. Their views, participation, and sensitivity can be ignored only at the peril of the future of Conservative Judaism. We have seen fit, after decades of agonizing debate, bitter polemics, and much soul-searching, that to exclude and disenfranchise 50% of our potential would be fool-hardy and self-destructive. We can only hope that the small groups of rabbis and cantors in our movement who disagree with this position will accept the pluralist options which we offer, and not defect to pseudo-orthodoxy.

These, then are the principles we stand for in Conservative Judaism:

1. Unflagging, unwavering support for the State of Israel — political, financial, emotional, religious, and in every other way possible. To be a Jew means to stand together with the people who guard the borders of Eretz Yisrael with firmness and loyalty and commitment. *"El artzi ve-el moladetee taylekh!"* (Gen. 24:4)
2. We stand by the ancient prophetic vision of justice and peace for all peoples — Palestinian and Israeli, Moslem and Jew . . . all God's chilren — in a Movement which must build synagogues characterized by compassion for the stranger, the orphan, the widow, the hungry, and the naked. Like Rebecca, we must do not only what we are asked, but even more than we are asked (Gen. 24:14).
3. We stand for a profound awareness of the participation of Almighty God in all matters. We are not here to build synagogues which have splendid New Year's Eve parties and lavish Sunday morning bagel and lox breakfasts with entertaining speakers. We want to help our members achieve a spiritual *Weltanschauung*, one which is always supported by the philosophy that *"May-Hashem yatzah ha-davar* — God is involved in our society and in our lives." (Gen. 24:50)
4. Last, our ideology is inclusive, not exclusive. This ideology brings all the elements of the modern family, wives, husbands, single parents, grandparents, and children into a large extended family which participates and shares equally in the decisions and celebrations of modern Jewish spiritual life. *"Nikrah la-naara ve-nishal et piha"* (Gen. 24:57).

We look forward to a renewal of Judaism based on these sacred principles that have stood our ancestors well from the days of Abraham and Sarah until this very hour. Our forbears have guarded this sacred trust devotedly, and we *dare not* do differently.

Part III:

Jewish Concerns and Institutions

THE JEWISH FAMILY

Golda Meir once said, "*Mishpacha achat kulanu*" (we are all one family). Family is the heart of the Jewish people. A recent Gallup Poll (Cleveland *Plain Dealer*, 2-26-89) shows the importance of the family in American life. On an 11-point scale, 9 out of 10 people (89%) assigned one of the top two positions to the importance of having a good family life. Close behind, 85% felt that having a good self-image and self-respect were second-most important, and 84% put good physical health in third place. Less important were a sense of accomplishment and lasting contribution (69%), working for betterment of American society (67%), and following a strict moral code (60%). What's amazing to me is that family was ranked higher than health, material goods, sense of accomplishment, and many other items.

11 Changes in the American Jewish Family

Many years ago a study by the American Jewish Committee discussed eleven changes in the American Jewish family (Boston *Jewish Advocate* (12-30-76). These changes are still relevant today.

1. "More Jews marry later than members of other groups."
25 years ago, young Jews married in their early 20's. My brother married at age 21, and when I waited til age 22, I was considered "late." Today, couples wait until their 30's. They have fewer children, later in life, not joining a synagogue until the children are old enough for Sunday School. Their involvement in the synagogue is delayed, and the span of affiliation is thus shortened. In addition, later marriages increase fertility problems, and adoption is becoming more common among Jews. Many Jewish agencies, however, no longer offer adoption services.

2. "Most Jewish singles groups no longer operate solely for the purpose of matching. These groups are now supportive of singles and the single way of life."
Are young Jews making a virtue out of a necessity? Is the single lifestyle the new alternative? Dr. Sylvia Barack Fishman, of Brandeis University, reports that "Only 20 years ago, the proportion of American Jewish singles - at 6% - lagged far behind the 16% of singles in the general American population; today, in many major metropolitan areas, between one-third to one-fifth of the adult Jewish population is single, exceeding the national average of 19%." (Washington D.C., for example, has one of the highest proportions of singles due to the high degree of mobility of people working for the government.)

In the Jewish community, marriage, family, and raising children were always the cornerstone. Childlessness reduces size of the Jewish community and is inimical to goals of Jewish survival. The degree of Jewish affiliation and volunteerism has diminished with the increased rate of singles and decrease in childbearing. In addition, the Jewish emphasis on family makes it very difficult for singles to find their place in the Jewish community. Jewish schools and synagogues must become much more sensitive to this problem. (Again, Washington, with many singles religious services and programs proliferating, is perhaps a model for single involvement.)

3. **"The divorce rate is rising. There appears to be no stigma for the failure of marriage and there is no presumption of permanence."**

Divorce in Judaism has always been considered the last alternative, a final step if continuing the marriage is impossible. Yet today people divorce too easily, developing a pattern of what Margaret Mead calls serial marriages. This attitude is reflected by a couple who came to me in pre-marital interview. They felt that they would be married not "till death do us part" but "until we stop loving each other." Further, though many have no objection to living together before marriage, I am not sure it helps. Many couples live together happily until marriage, then break up.

One major problem in Jewish education is that we provide no training for marriage. Freud maintained that the two most important choices in life are one's career and one's mate. School does not provide training for marriage, thus Jewish family life education becomes vital. Basic to marriage training is learning to communicate: we can communicate with people in Beijing or Haifa by dialing the phone; watch what's happening in Teheran or Jerusalem, on TV live; but we still can't talk to our families across the dinner table. We need to teach these special skills.

A second problem with divorce involves blended families. Traditionally, Halachah dictates that at a Bar Mitzvah, two brothers are not allowed successive aliyot. Why worry about halachic problems when we now must decide which father precedes which at the Torah? Rabbi Harold Schulweis states that the Bar/Bat Mitzvah is becoming less a rite of passage into adolescence than traumatic passage into living without 2 parents. I know of a story in which an adopted child found his birth-father. His adoptive father had divorced, thus three fathers were at the Bar Mitzvah: the birth father, adoptive father, and the step-father.

The current trends in family life emphasize the need for Jewish family life education. Public schools used to teach children from immigrant homes what parents couldn't teach. Today parents are consumers, selecting schools, becoming active in PTA. Yet, Jewish schools still deal with families as if they are outside the educational loop. We need to bring them in. As Mordecai Kaplan said, "Teaching children without parents is like trying to heat a home while leaving the windows open." We have a great need for Jewish family educators. Our regular teachers in the classroom have not been trained in the special skills needed for this new and increasingly important kind of Jewish education.

The diagnosis of the Jewish family is Mishpachitis. Therapy requires a course in menschology.

4. "The birthrate is falling and childlessness has become socially acceptable."

A recent study from Brandeis University states that we are losing a generation every 30 years, because couples have fewer children due to late marriages; women marrying in their 30's often experience infertility; the fertility rate for Jewish women is 1.5 children, as opposed to the average national rate of 1.9. Jews have always been in the forefront of social movements, and Zero Population Growth (ZPG) is no exception. We are the wrong segment of the community to be concerned about ZPG, having lost 1/3 of our people in the last generation. In 1939, there were 18 million Jews in world, today we number 12 million. The Jewish population should be 20 or 30 million.

In Gloria Goldreich's novel, *The Four Days*, one of the women debates whether she should go through with her pregnancy. Her mother, a Holocaust survivor, says to her: "Every Jewish baby that is born is a slap in Hitler's face." Along the same lines, philosopher Emil Fackenheim wrote that Jews have an "11th commandment: Thou Shalt Survive! Thou shalt not give Hitler a posthumous victory!"

5. "Financial success rather than the rearing of children has become for many the major goal of the family."

Rabbi Schulweis feels that Jews still want their children to be doctors and lawyers, but not for traditional Jewish goals of healing and bringing justice. Instead, they want their children to gain prestige, material security. It seems that some parents even consider nursery school to be part of college preparation. God forbid the child is refused entry in the best school - s/he won't get into medical school. Rabbi Schulweis continues:

> When they say "Larry is a good boy," they invariably mean that he does whatever is necessary to bring home the extrinsic, external marks, the grade A. Goodness no longer means what it meant in the Jewish value system in phrases like a gute mensch, a sheine Yid. It doesn't refer to character, it refers only to the external tokens of a society which says this is the mark of success. Goodness in middle classism means success. And the greater secular sin is not derived from the litany of Al Chet on Yom Kippur, with coarseness of spirit and exploitation and insularity and selfishness and lack of concern. The greatest secular sin is failure: economic failure, marital failure, academic failure. Sin for Jeff is to bring home a C or a D, and venial sin, an F.

A recent special edition of *Newsweek* devoted to family contained an interesting insight; youth become expert consumers long before they become producers. In other words, we give them too many valuables, not enough values. One university researcher called it "premature affluence." No longer is the Jewish family held out as model as it once was. Today, families of Asian immigrants are exemplified as stressing a culture in which "strong family systems where the notions of activity, responsibility and work are values."

6. **"The degree and intensity of family interaction has decreased, although it continues to be higher than that of other religious and ethnic groups."**

A study showed that the average parent talks directly to his or her child 7 minutes per week. Someone once said, "My father spoke Yiddish, I spoke English, yet we understood each other. Now, I speak English, my son speaks English, but we can't communicate!"

In many families, both parents work hard outside the home, and spend little quality time at home with the family. My answer is Shabbat, my favorite theme in Jewish teaching and observance. Friday night at home can become a sacred time. Achad Ha-Am said, "More than the Jews have kept Shabbat, the Shabbat has kept the Jewish People." At least one night a week, the family interacts. I have always admired the Kennedy household, about which it was said that Papa Kennedy would not let the children come to the table without some current event from the day's newspaper. In the Jewish home, on Friday night the family can discuss Jewish problems or the weekly Sidrah.

Another obstacle to family communication is television. The average American child watches 7 hours a day. TV destroys imagination and creativity, and limits reading and family interaction. Video games, VCRs, Nintendo, and a TV in every room are turning this generation into passive people. Dr. Alvin Schiff, head of Jewish education in New York City, notes that "upon graduation from high school, the average American teenager will have spent many more hours in front of the tube than in school." With the strongest influences in our children's lives being from the environment rather than their own family, how can we as Jews transmit what is sacred to us? What happens to family values — to Shabbat, commitment, loyalty, concern for Israel, Jewish people, Jewish learning? All of these are derived from family interaction.

The *Newsweek* "Family" issue warns us that "What the young see enshrined in the media and malls of America are, after all, the values adults put there: consumerism, narcissism, and the instant gratification of desire. When those change, so will American youth."

7. **"There is less socialization across generational lines, partly as a result of geographic mobility."**

Mobility is one of the most serious problems facing the family. Generations grow up apart from each other. Demographic patterns, known as "polarization by age," profoundly influence generational interaction. Families with young children usually live in suburban areas; childless couples find themselves in urban areas; and the elderly move to communities specifically designed for their needs, or else are left behind in less affluent urban neighborhoods devoid of Jewish youth. No place remains for intergenerational encounter.

Generational polarization means that support systems disappear. Young families no longer have the support systems of nearby older relatives. So much is lost due to the lack of older role models: for example learning about Yiddishkeit, the old country, illness, dying, and mourning rites. Our kids settle around the country and around the world.

8. "The sense of responsibility of individual family members to other family members has decreased."

This trend occurred in my own family. At the celebration of my oldest son Hillel's becoming a Bar Mitzvah in 1976, the whole family was present. Two year's later, fewer came to Jonathan's simcha. My youngest daughter, Shira, counted on one hand the number of family members who attended her Bat Mitzvah. In addition, families do not get together as much on the holidays. How many come home for Seder? It used to be the whole mishpachah. However, in recent years, community Sedarim have grown in popularity. People have nowhere to go, and families don't or can't travel. Synagogue bulletins carry articles encouraging people to host families for those with no Seder to attend. These developments point toward a need for Havurot, which can function as substitute extended families.

9. "The rule of Jewishness is no longer central to the lives of many individual family members."

Psychoanalyst Dr. Carl Jung found that in patients over 40, the main problem was a lack of meaning in life due to an absence of a religious outlook. Jewish educator Dr. Alvin Schiff tells us that the most critical challenge we face as a Jewish community results from changes in living styles, best described by the term, a "many more generation":

> Today, more Jews are eating glatt kosher; many more are not eating kosher at all.
> More Jews pray every day, 3 times a day; many more do not pray at all.
> More Jews make kiddush on Friday night; many more do not observe Shabbat at all.
> More Jews study Talmud — *Daf yomi* — every day; many more have no relationship to Jewish learning at all, never read a Jewish book.

Rabbi Harold Schulweis notes that Jews are becoming "seventh-day absentists." Explains Schulweis: They are revolving door Jews, in on Rosh Hashanah, out on Yom Kippur — they who own tokens of affiliation, four tickets, center aisle, and see the synagogue as theatre. Their exposure to the rabbi is limited to occasional rites to which they come with impatience, to be hatched, matched and dispatched (birth, marriage, funeral).

We could discuss for hours the results of the absence of the Jewish rhythm in the life of today's Jews, such as the increase in alcoholism, drug abuse, AIDS, juvenile delinquency, divorce, crime, wife and child abuse . . . things which never used to be present in the Jewish community. We need to meet these needs and many other contemporary problems.

Jewish education is a failing enterprise in most communities and congregations, because the two most powerful influences on children are environment and family, followed by the school. With absence of Jewishness, Jewish values, learning, and commitment in the environment and in the family, the school works with its hands tied behind its back. Only when the goals of the school and the home are in synch can the school succeed. Unfortunately, that is rarely the case.

Therefore, we need to turn our Religious Schools into places of education for the entire Jewish family, and stop thinking of Jewish education as something for the *kinder*. Dr. Alvin Schiff recommends that a new child-family focus must be created in Jewish education, implying a restructuring of the synagogue such that the rabbi, education director, teachers, cantor, and youth leaders work as family educator teams.

10. **"Intermarriage has resulted in a lessening of involvement of the Jewish partner in Jewish life and less emphasis on the Jewish aspects of family events."**

The growing rate of intermarriage remains of vital interest to the Jewish family. Samson Raphael Hirsch notes, "Every intermarriage is another nail in the coffin of Judaism." The intermarriage rate ranges from 25 - 50%, depending on the region of the country and the size of the Jewish community. Even the Orthodox are not immune to this problem.

Regarding intermarriage, new halachic questions arise. The Rabbinical Assembly Committee on Law and Jewish Standards asked in a recent "*She-elah*": "Should synagogues congratulate members upon the marriage of their children to non-Jews? What is the propriety of congratulating the grandparents of a newborn when the child's parents are intermarried?" Various decisions of the Committee in the 1970's were cited: The synagogue may not congratulate intermarried couple in the synagogue bulletin. However, when a child is born, if the mother is Jewish, and the child is not being raised in another faith, a congratulatory notice may appear in the bulletin. When the mother is not Jewish, the CJLS was evenly split regarding acknowledgement in the bulletin.

Over the past three decades, parents' attitudes towards intermarriage have changed. The following statistics from a survey done in 1965 in Boston speak for themselves. In 1965, 26% of parents polled strong opposed intermarriage. By 1985, the number strongly opposed dropped to 9%! In l965, 44% of parents reported that they would discourage a child's intermarriage; in 1985, that proportion dropped to 22%! In 1965 25% said they would be neutral or accept intermarriage; in 1985, 66% would be neutral or accept! An even newer study shows that parental opposition to intermarriage has eroded even further, especially when children are 35 and over.

11. An eleventh change in Jewish life is the emergence of feminism and changing sex roles.

In 1981, 47 million American women were working outside the home, as compared to 32 million in 1970. This is about a 50% increase in little over 10 years. Of women in the labor force, one in six are sole providers in their family. The pressures on the single working parent are enormous. Further, more women choose the "career track" over the "Mommy Track," in which mothers combine their career with raising children. For women who want to find personal and professional self-fulfillment, modern families must make many adjustments. We need to come to terms with a new reality. Our kids are lonely after school, with no parents at home and less of a sense of neighborhood, and hard-working parents have less quality time for them.

Child-rearing has changed drastically in the last two decades. A recent study showed that 62% of American mothers of pre-school children were employed outside the home. This is a tenfold increase since World War II! In the next few years, 75% of mothers with pre-school children will be working outside the home. Day-care must become a national priority so working women and single parents can function with peace of mind.

To solve these serious problems of the contemporary Jewish family we must set our minds and hearts, or we shall have no future.

WHO NEEDS A SYNAGOGUE ANYWAY?

Chuck Ratner, a major figure in the Cleveland Jewish community, made a profound comment on the role of the synagogue in Jewish life (at a previous meeting of the series at which this talk was delivered). Chair of a Federation campaign that raises $25 million (the largest per capita Jewish giving in the world), his family gives the largest Ohio-area gift to the Federation and one of largest gifts in world. Here were his words: "The Synagogue is the *neshama* of Jewish life."

A popular folk saying from the Zohar maintains that *Eretz Yisrael blee Torah hee ke-guf blee neshama* (The Land of Israel without Torah is like a body without a soul). I think we can expand the literal meaning of Eretz Yisrael to mean "Jewish nationalism." Jewish cultural life without religion or Torah is like a body without a soul. This is precisely what Chuck meant. Expanding on his statement, *guf bli neshama* (a body without a soul) is dead. Jewish life without a soul would be a lifeless body. The problem is that too many people think they can live without the synagogue, in part because of the many thriving substitutes. In fact, the very title of this presentation indicates that some people question whether we really do need a synagogue today, with so many other successful Jewish community institutions?

Organization of Present Jewish Community

One of major weaknesses in Jewish life is that it is disorganized, confused, and splintered. Purposes of various institutions overlap and boundaries are blurred. The synagogue is the basic *community* institution in Jewish life. No other institution is indispensable. The synagogue has three traditional roles — *Bet Knesset*, *Bet Midrash*, and *Bet Tefilah*.

A) *Bet Knesset* (House of Assembly):
Some of these functions are performed by other institutions (primarily the JCC, but also Hadassah, ORT, B'nai B'rith, etc.) which also serve social and service functions.

B) *Bet Midrash* (House of Study):
Community education on all levels is provided by the College of Jewish Studies, the Federation, the JCC, the Bureau of Jewish Education, Cleveland Hebrew Schools, day schools, etc. However, the primary delivery system of youth education in the Jewish community is the synagogue, including the Sunday School and the afternoon Hebrew School. Even day schools are in large measure a product of the synagogue, and many are supported by synagogue movements.

C) *Bet Tefilah* (House of Prayer):
No other institution can replace this synagogue function. The reverse is not true — that the synagogue cannot replace any other institution.

The function of the synagogue as a *Bet Tefilah* has never been replaced, and never will be, including the spiritual leadership which goes along with it — rabbi, hazzan, shamash, etc. Unless the Jewish community is willing to do without Shabbat and Festival services, bar/bat mitzvahs, confirmation, weddings, funerals, and other life cycle and calendar celebrations, the synagogue will remain the focal institution in Jewish life.

The Synagogue's role as *Bet Tefilah* also encompasses the roles of *Bet Knesset* and *Bet Midrash*, because in truth each part is integral to the whole. At Shabbat and Festival worship, there must be a strong sense of *klal yisrael*, a tightly knit community, which not only sings, meditates and prays, but also listens to the Torah reading, the sermon, the devar Torah, the Bar/Bat Mitzvah address, the prayers for the sick, the bride and groom, birthdays and other milestone events — mostly in Hebrew. This becomes one of the significant study periods during the life of the regular worshipper. In other words, each of the synagogue's three roles reinforces and strengthens the others. None of these roles can be totally separated from the other two.

Other Institutions' Roles

Three other major Jewish community institutions now effectively fulfill other roles.

A) Tzedakah — Federation
The synagogue teaches the importance of tzedakah through the Religious School, the pulpit, and adult Jewish education. Rabbinic support is vital for community backing of the Federation.

B) Community (*Bet Knesset*) — JCC
The synagogue provides the shared values and cultural and religious norms which form the basis for the sense of community which invigorates the JCC. Without the shared heritage, culture, religion, value system, and languages, which the synagogue keeps alive, the JCC would be just another health club where people come to lose weight or keep trim.

C) Israel
Even the State of Israel would not be as significant a draw for world Jewry without the Torah as its national repository of our cultural and religious birthright. Does the Mideast need one more nation-state? Most countries think not — and if not to preserve Jewish spiritual values, then why maintain a Jewish state altogether? In the future, after the Soviet, Ethiopian, and other refugee Jewish communities are safely transplanted in Israel, thus negating the need for Israel to function as a refuge for world Jewry, what would the Diaspora Jewish community have to live for? The answer is one thing, and one thing alone: preservation of the Jewish heritage and its moral and spiritual values. No other

institution can preserve these by itself!

Preserving our Heritage

The synagogue is vital to a substantial Jewish identity. Without its influence, the Jewish heritage would be reduced to lox and bagels, Jewish humor, and rallies for the survival of Israel. We require the supremacy of Jewish values such as learning, ethics, marking life cycle milestones with meaningful ceremonies and rituals, and a historical consciousness that ties us to the search for God and the good life, from Abraham and Sarah to our own day. Otherwise, there is absolutely no raison d'etre for the continuity of the Jewish People.

Back in 1917, Rabbi Mordecai M. Kaplan said (and it still holds true today), "In this country, as well as in all other countries where the Jews have been emancipated, the synagogue is the principal means of keeping alive the Jewish consciousness. . . . (It) is the only institution which can define our aims to a world that would otherwise be at a loss to understand why we persist in retaining our corporate individuality."

The synagogue, and the synagogue alone, is capable of preserving our 4000 year old heritage.

GIVING FORM TO OUR IMAGINATION:
THE SYNAGOGUE SCHOOL IN THE 21st CENTURY

I had completed a long list of ideas for the Synagogue School of the 21st Century, and was about to sit down and write my paper, (for the annual conference sponsored by the Council for Jewish Education), when I glanced upon the Spring-Summer 1990 issue of *Jewish Education*. Lo and behold, the pieces by Alvin Schiff and Rela Geffen Monson under the title "Toward the Year 2000" contained everything I had written down. Therefore, instead of compiling a list of the familiar innovations in Jewish education and pasting them up into a perfected picture of a 20th century school, I decided to branch out a bit and let my imagination take me wherever it wanted to go. I came up with three ideas. Since we all agree with Kohelet that "*Ayn kol hadash tachat ha-shamesh*" (there's nothing new under the sun) I'm not even sure that these ideas are that far out. Surely if I were to read past issues of Jewish educational journals, I would find something similar to what I am now about to present.

Enlarged Framework

First, synagogue education in the 21st century will need an enlarged framework. Instead of thinking of a "synagogue school" at which children from Kindergarten through 12th grade study, we must consider the entire synagogue as a place of growth and learning for the whole family and community. The educational process contains far too much potential to be contained within the four walls of a classroom. As the philosopher Santayana once put it, "A child educated only at school is an uneducated child."

Not only will the school/synagogue of the 21st century have to more fiercely break out of the classroom, it will have to break out of the mold of strictly cognitive learning, which a limited number of educational programs have now begun to do. The horizons of Jewish learning will embrace all aspects of personality, including cognitive, affective, and spiritual domains. The job of the educator in the 21st century will be not to teach or train, but to help the learner grow as a Jew and as a human being. To paraphrase my late teacher, Rabbi Abraham Joshua Heschel, we want to make young people into Jews, and we also want to make young Jews into people.

In a passage explaining what the Torah means when Moshe tells God that he is not an eloquent speaker and therefore not an adequate leader to take B'nai Yisrael out of Egypt, the Midrash debated over the root of the word *moreh* (teacher). God allays Moshe's fears by telling him that he will <u>teach</u> him what to say: "*ve-horayteekha asher tedaber*" (Exodus 4:14). Rabbi Abahu explains the root of *ve-horayteekha* as *yara*, to shoot an arrow. God will put the words in the mouth of Moshe as an archer shoots his arrows into the target. But then Rabbi Shimon insists that *ve-horayteekha* comes not from *yara* but from *hara*, to give birth. In Rabbi Shimon's words, "*Boray ani otekha beriah hadasha*" (I will make a new creature of you) (Midrash, Exodus Rabba). The teacher of the 21st century will not be one who shoots arrows, or who deposits information, but rather one who helps create new human beings, who sees his/her task as the formation of a healthy, whole, mature, humanized person whose Jewish wisdom infuses the mind, heart and soul.

Individualized Education

Second, the educational program of the synagogue in the 21st century will be much more democratized and individualized, on the order of the Montessori School. Instead of a boiler-plate programmed curriculum, the synagogue would provide a wide variety of choices. A child's Jewish education would be tailor-made under the tutelage of a guide, mentor, teacher, or rabbi. The individualized program would be agreed upon by the entire family, together with the guide, because the learning program of the 21st century school will be family-oriented, not child-oriented. It would be forged by the family together with the guide, and sealed with a learning contract, which would then be the basis of a future evaluation of its effectiveness.

The family might be able to choose from a menu of learning tasks under different subject areas such as Bible, Hebrew language, history, literature, liturgy, Zionism, spiritual growth, *menschlichkeit*, etc. Learning vehicles would be extremely diverse, including formal classes, seminars and workshops, private instruction, research papers, writing in personal spiritual diaries, participation as well as leadership in daily, Shabbat and Festival worship, attendance at public lectures, individual and family reading, extensive use of audio- and video-tapes, radio and TV programs, Shabbatonim, interviews with famous personalities, the creation of family genealogies, home discussions, community courses, public service, travel experiences at home and abroad, etc.

The Role of Life-Cycle Events

Third, and last, I see the school/synagogue of the 21st century utilizing life-cycle events to a much greater degree. Consecration, Bar/Bat Mitzvah, Confirmation and graduation — the four developmental stages of the educational process from grades K-12, should be opportunities for families to teach their children how to grow from one developmental task to the next.

Instead of the school preparing children to participate in a public ceremony, the family must be guided and nurtured so that they can lead their child from one stage of life's growth process to the next. Bar/Bat Mitzvah training, for example, would include teaching the parents how to use the tallit and tefillin so that they can teach their offspring, instead of the school training the child directly. Education for Shabbat would not only include teaching the kiddush in the classroom, but having the parents learn the Shabbat rituals so that they can transmit them to their family in the natural setting of the home. From one life-cycle milestone to the next, the family will be educated to lead its young through the various stages of its own evolution. The family will examine its value system, belief structure, observance level, community commitment, and its determination of where that family fits into the Jewish community, the Jewish People, and Jewish history.

With new creative possibilities such as these — the expansion of the educational process from the classroom to the entire congregation so that the growth of each member is enhanced and his/her potential realized, the individualization of the educational process to meet the family's needs and goals, and finally, the marshalling of the family's inner resources to move through the stages of growth and development as a family — hopefully the school/synagogue of the 21st century will fulfill the ancient prophecy of Joel (1:3):

> Tell your children of it,
> And let your children tell their children,
> And their children will pass it on to another generation.

MY VIEW OF JEWISH EDUCATION

The first people who influenced me to enter the field of Jewish education were the rabbi and teachers at the Beth Sholom synagogue in Philadelphia, Pennsylvania, who nurtured my love for Judaism, the Jewish People, and Jewish learning in the congregational school at which I studied from ages five through fifteen.

My earliest teachers, Ruth DeWolf, Ephraim Goldman, and Isadore Glassman, in addition to my spiritual mentor, Rabbi Mortimer J. Cohen, exercised a most profound influence on my life. I came from a typical Conservative Jewish home, with no kashrut or Shabbat observance, and little knowledge of things Jewish. These teachers took me under their wing and shepherded me through the ranks of the Religious School and Youth Program, so that I became president of the high school youth group (USY), valedictorian of the Confirmation Class, and was then encouraged to continue my studies at Gratz College toward a diploma in Jewish education.

At Gratz a large group of fine scholars and devoted educators saw my potential and steered me into the field of professional Jewish life. These included Professors Sidney Fish, Daniel Isaacman, Ezra Shereshevsky, Joseph Levitsky, Leon Leibreich, Nahum Sarna, Shlomo Dov Goitein, Samuel Pitlik, and most of all William and Elsie Chomsky. I studied at Gratz during eleventh and twelfth grades in high school, and for the first three years of college, after which time I received a diploma in Hebrew studies and Jewish education. At Gratz, the atmosphere of excitement about Jewish life, Zionism, Jewish scholarship and the burgeoning field of Jewish education, was contagious.

While at Gratz I became the protege of Will and Elsie Chomsky, and was appointed as a student-teacher at the Gratz College School of Observation and Practice. Under the close weekly supervision of Elsie Chomsky and the broader direction of Dr. William Chomsky (whose courses I was taking in the importance of literary Hebrew as a vehicle for teaching and learning), I made my first forays into the realities of the front lines of Jewish education.

During the summers in the last three years of Gratz I also attended Camp Ramah in Pennsylvania's beautiful Pocono mountains as a cabin counselor and division supervisor (rosh aydah). At Ramah I was deeply inspired by the new experiments in Jewish education promoted by the Jewish Theological Seminary's Teachers' Institute, under the direction of Rabbi Seymour Fox and Sylvia Ettenberg. Through five summers at Camp Ramah I was exposed to the religious and educational philosophies of prominent Jewish educators such as

---

I wrote this paper at the request of the Jewish Educational Service of N. America (JESNA), after having been nominated for their prestigious Covenant Award.

Louis Newman, Levi Soshuk, Aryeh Rohn, Rabbi David Mogilner, Rabbi Alexander Shapiro, Matthew Mosenkis, Dr. William Lakritz, Bezalel Porten, Leon Spotts, Raphael Arzt, and by the deep Jewish scholarship of such people as Professors David Halivni-Weiss, Zvi Ankori, Gerson D. Cohen, and Yosef Yerushalmi.

Ramah was a hothouse for experimentation in progressive Jewish education, oscillating among the educational theories of John Dewey, Mordecai M. Kaplan, Joseph Schwab, Isaac Berkson, and others. There were serious attempts at education of the whole child, including moral education, democratic community (elective classes and activities), and it was there, I believe, that the first seeds of my later involvement in experiential learning took root. It was Dewey's notion of learning by doing, and learning through the classroom of life, that profoundly affected my path and career in Jewish education in later years.

The residue of my Ramah experience was a profound commitment to the ever-growing process of Jewish education that would contain elements of the formal and the informal, learning through structured experiences, learning as a living, vibrant aspect of a total living community, learning as a lifelong process of moral growth and development, and education as a fulfilling way of life (*Torah lish'ma*). Nothing I have been involved with in the field of Jewish education since the late 1950's, and my five remarkable summers at Camp Ramah, has been devoid of a powerful component of Ramah experience and philosophy.

Upon graduation from Temple University, where I majored in literature, I matriculated at the Rabbinical School of the Jewish Theological Seminary (JTS) (1959-1964), and was further influenced in my knowledge of the field of Jewish education by the teachings of Professor Simon Greenberg and Dr. Abraham Ezra Millgram. In my first year at JTS, I participated in a select seminar in Jewish education taught by Seymour Fox, whose energy, creative vision, charisma, and excitement about bringing the best of the field of general education into the Jewish community was an extraordinary learning experience. His careful study with us of the works of Harry Stack Sullivan, seminal psychiatric thinker of the 1940s, began my long process of integrating the insights of human development and education, and connecting the study and practice of Judaism to the broader process of creating the fully-functioning self-actualizing person.

During my Seminary years I was also deeply involved with a now-defunct group known as Leaders Training Fellowship, an arm of the Teachers Institute of the JTS. LTF was a national organization for the cream of high school youth in the Conservative Movement. As assistant national director of LTF during two of my Seminary years, I became increasingly aware of the important role of the congregational rabbi as a potential molder of high school youth through the synagogue youth program, and of how some of the ideas I was exposed to at Ramah could be translated into congregational life. I saw what enormous impact rabbis and educators can have on young impressionable personalities, to bring a powerful dimension of intense Jewish commitment to the future leaders of the Jewish community.

During four of my five years at the Seminary, I also taught in various Sunday and Hebrew Schools in the New York area, including one under the auspices of the Melton Center for Jewish Education. The Melton emphasis on character education, open discussion in the classroom, freedom of inquiry, and the search for meaning — even in younger grades —- were good training for my later work in the field.

A chance experience during my first Seminary year brought me into close contact with Dr. Azriel Eisenberg, then Director of the Jewish Education Committee of New York (now known as the Board of Jewish Education). After I reviewed one of Dr. Eisenberg's children's books on biblical archeology, he invited me to collaborate on his next book. I accepted the invitation with great excitement, and began a relationship that lasted until his death 25 years later. Eisenberg's close friendship and tutelage brought me into the world of the classic Jewish educators of the first half of the 20th century. The writings and ideas on Jewish education of such educational giants as Samson Benderly, Alexander Dushkin, Louis Katzoff, Shlomo Bardin, Samuel Dinin, Leo Honor, Emanuel Gamoran, Louis Kaplan, Albert Schoolman, Judah Pilch and other creative pioneers became familiar topics of discussion and correspondence. I cannot exaggerate the important impact that this learned, dynamic educator had upon my life. The significance of spoken Hebrew, the use of traditional and modern literature as focal points in the classroom, the dearth of usable material for classroom teachers, and the importance of day school education, all were deeply impressed on me as major themes for future work through my contact with Azriel Eisenberg. Through his influence writing became one of my major vehicles for transmission of ideas in work in Jewish education. The two books on biblical archeology I wrote with Dr. Eisenberg, two other teen books I later published (stories about Jewish chaplains in the American military, and a biography of Rabbi Abraham Isaac Kook) and the many books of experiential exercises and value clarification programs for teachers and group leaders which I wrote, were all enriched by the criticisms and suggestions which he made before publication.

At JTS I was privileged to be exposed to many great minds, but none had greater impact than Mordecai M. Kaplan and Abraham Joshua Heschel. Primarily known as Jewish philosophers and theologians, both also had great influence on the rapidly developing field of Jewish education. Kaplan's notions of democracy and relevance in contemporary Jewish life, the synagogue-center where all of one's social, cultural and religious needs were met, and his framework of the organic, caring community foreshadowed the later work of Lawrence Kohlberg of Harvard. I became steeped in the Kaplanian approach to make Judaism important to scientifically-oriented, modern-thinking Jews. Kaplan's summary statement on Jewish education was that trying to teach a child in the absence of a supportive family and community is like trying to heat a house while keeping the windows open. My emphasis on family-oriented Jewish education has been the result, in part, of this teaching.

Professor Abraham Joshua Heschel's influence continues even until the present moment. Heschel's mystical bent, his love of Hasidism and the joy it brought to worship and Jewish living, and his passionate devotion to social justice (which came from his reading of and writing about, the biblical prophets) are among my important and primary preoccupations of late, more so now than ever before in my career in Jewish life. I have always been a strong advocate of freedom for Soviet Jewry and other oppressed communities, as well as for African Americans, Jewish and non-Jewish women, and all others who lack the right of full enfranchisement and participation in modern secular and religious life.

I was an early advocate of greater public activism for Soviet Jewry, and wrote several articles for *The American Zionist* in the late '60's on this theme. I was Federation chair of the committee for Soviet Jewry in Jacksonville, Florida and in Rochester, N.Y., during the '70's, and travelled to the Soviet Union in October, 1988, following which I published a diary of my experience titled *My Seventy-Two Friends: Encounters with Jews in the USSR*. In January, 1991 I travelled to Ethiopia, and have recently been writing and speaking on this theme throughout the Cleveland area as well as nationally. My preaching and teaching constantly reflect the theme of prophetic justice as a model for humanity. As Heschel was wont to repeat, Jewish life desperately needs more text *persons* (human role models whose lives and ideas influence their students) even more than new text *books*.

From 1976-1984 I temporarily left the pulpit and served as an independent educational consultant and trainer to rabbis, synagogues, educators, bureaus of Jewish education and Jewish community federations through an organization I founded called Growth Associates. During this time I underwent additional training in organizational development, humanistic education, group dynamics, human resource development, family systems, and family counseling at scores of day-long, week-long, and year-long in-service seminars at such institutions and growth centers, and other graduate study programs as University Associates, NTL (National Training Labs), Esalen Institute, the Gestalt Institute of Cleveland, led by many of the world's leading facilitators of human growth and development.

I consider myself extremely fortunate to have been exposed over the past five decades to great men and women of deep learning, vision, insight, creativity, and courage who have broken new ground in the fields of Jewish and general education. The contributions I have been able to make myself in these areas are due to their influence and my own personal calling to enrich and enhance their legacy.

I have been involved in Jewish education since my high school days, my experience spanning almost four decades. During this time I have achieved a philosophy of Jewish education, and have enough experience in the field to have a fairly clear picture of what I am aiming for.

After several years of rabbinical service, I began to perceive a theoretical framework into which my contribution to Jewish education could be made. I formulated a plan which included a series of concentric circles of influence in the field of Jewish education. Each congregational religious school is a sub-system of a larger system, the congregation at large. In turn, the congregation is a sub-system of a larger system of the national Conservative Movement. The Conservative Movement in turn is a sub-system of the world-wide family of the Jewish People. Being influential in each sub-system is important, but the higher the level of influence, or the larger the concentric circle one occupies, the greater the opportunity for influence for system-wide development and change. Being a congregational rabbi permits me to influence the school, the youth program, family educational programs, adult education, and every other aspect of Jewish education in the congregation, creating an opportunity for a coordinated, community-centered, family-oriented approach to Jewish growth.

In the field of Jewish education, I hope to achieve the creation of a successful model of a synagogue which places education as the highest priority and the central focus of its congregational agenda. Such education will differ from what is available in synagogues today in that it will reflect a unique philosophy of education and an integrated, holistic system of formal and informal, youth and adult, individual and family learning, with a strong emphasis on not only preserving the Jewish cultural and spiritual heritage, but also the enrichment of the personal and professional lives of those involved in this educational process. In the words of Rabbi Abraham Joshua Heschel, we want to make Jews out of human beings, and human beings out of Jews.

The model of human nature I work with flows from my training in humanistic psychology and parallels the Jewish view of the person as an ever growing, changing and developing creature with potential far beyond that which any of us has yet achieved. As Pirke Avot put it so succinctly, *de-la moseef yasef*, either growth or death. For growth to sustain itself, it must be reinforced by the environment. Thus, a successful model of Jewish learning in a congregation must reflect the involvement of the entire system.

The teachers, students, and curriculum of such a learning environment must be integrated such that the entire congregation becomes a learning community. The lines between formal and informal, classroom, home learning and less structured programs should be carefully coordinated to achieve our educational goals. Such a program of integrated system-wide learning will include active and intensive parent involvement in the school, outside-of-school total family experiences such as kallot, Shabbatonim, day-long outings, havurot (the "mishpacha" model I developed and have written about in my book, *Humanizing Jewish Life*), multi-family worship, festival celebrations, intergenerational seminars and workshops, etc.

Learning in this total-system approach will be both cognitive and affective, educating the mind, the heart and the soul. It will include factual information, but will also strive toward attitude building, emotional expression and commitment, character building, ethical sensitivity and constant searching for the highest moral path, as well as toward a spiritual journey that includes times for quiet thought, meditation, prayer, spiritual joy, celebration and even religious ecstasy. Furthermore, such learning will be both didactic and experiential. The main thrust of my own training, research, writing and experience is in education which includes learning through doing as well as through reading and listening. This is the approach of the four teacher/facilitator handbooks on experiential learning which I wrote between 1977 and 1979: (*Clarifying Jewish Values, Jewish Consciousness Raising, Experiential Programs for Jewish Groups*, and *Loving My Jewishness*).

My trust in the process of learning through living comes from a wide variety of sources, including the theoretical base of the writings of John Dewey, Abraham Maslow, Malcolm Knowles and others, training I have undergone by leaders in the general educational field such as Sidney B. Simon, Howard Kirschenbaum, Merrill Harmin, William Schutz, John Jones, William Pfeiffer, Carl R. Rogers, Joseph Zinker, Jack Canfield, Steve Andreas and many others, as well as long involvement in Camp Ramah, weekend retreats in Jewish and general groups, and related learning experiences. I do not see this type of affective/experiential learning as replacing book knowledge, but rather as an indispensable element in the overall process of learning.

I strongly believe that what I bring to the field of Jewish education in my multifaceted background in general education, humanistic psychology, pastoral counseling, group dynamics, family therapy and systems theory, makes me uniquely qualified to create the kind of institution-wide educational program that I am describing.

I derived enormous satisfaction from the pioneering efforts I was involved in at my former congregation, Beth El Temple of Rochester, NY, where I first experimented with havurah groups (we had more than 20 going at once), with family cluster groups (taught to me by Margaret Sawin, author of *Family Enrichment with Family Clusters*), and the course work I took in family life education with my doctoral advisor and mentor, Professor Edward E. Thornton, then at Colgate Rochester Divinity School.

I have continued this process of creating small groups such as, such as havurot, in my present congregation, The Park Synagogue, of Cleveland Heights, Ohio. In the almost four years I have been at Park we have made major strides in the directions which I have described above. We have engaged a Program Coordinator, a committed Conservative Jew with an M.S.W. She has created, under my supervision, 15 havurah groups, a senior citizens program, an extensive singles program, a mitzvah corps (lay volunteers trained to pay shiva calls, make hospital visits, and provide other para-rabbinic pastoral services), a bereavement group for widows and widowers, a Shabbaton program for various school classes and affiliate groups, and a home training program which teaches people how to create a traditional, meaningful Shabbat observance in the home on Friday nights. Our Shabbat morning and festival worship has become much more participatory, education-focused, and family-oriented. Our nursery school and day camp have intensified their Jewish curricula and involve parents and whole families in the educational process. We now send almost 50 children to Hebrew day schools, 25 to Camp Ramah, a dozen or more to Israel in summer- and semester-long programs, and are in the process of establishing an outreach program to families and couples who are intermarried or who include Jews-by-choice.

All of the above in some way include components of experiential learning, total-family involvement, and personal-growth oriented character education. Our full-time education director has charge of both our religious school and youth program, and is in full accord with my vision of a system-wide educational program. We have begun to lay the groundwork for a part- or full-time family life education staff person for the near future.

It is conventional wisdom that congregational education is not among the most successful ventures in Jewish life. In fact, the opposite is the case. We are far from reversing that dismal trend, but have made great strides in creating the kind of learning community that has the potential to create completely new models, and make a major shift forward in the effort to make congregational education a viable and successful enterprise.

We are supported in our efforts at Park Synagogue by a Jewish Community Federation that has invested large sums of money in many creative and innovative programs to raise the level of religious school, day school and retreat education, as well as in teacher recruitment and training. Our Bureau of Jewish Education and the Cleveland College of Jewish Studies have extensive pre- and in-service teacher training programs which give us major support toward our goals, and the Jewish Community Center has a newly-created Judaic department headed by several talented and innovative individuals who work with us in the development of our informal education and Shabbaton programs.

The will, resources, creative energy and pioneering spirit are present today in the Cleveland Jewish community, as well as at Park Synagogue, to cooperate in the implementation of my conception of a congregation that will continue to create new models of excellence in the field of Jewish education. I am thrilled to assist in providing the theoretical base, the vision and the leadership to help it come to pass.

CHAIM SHEL B'RACHA

In Celebration of a Group Wedding for Former Russian Jews

This morning in the Hallel Psalms of Praise, we recited the following words: "This is the day the Lord hath made. On it we shall rejoice and be glad." It is with this special feeling of *simcha*, rejoicing, that we celebrate the wedding of 25 Soviet Jewish couples at The Park Synagogue (Cleveland, Ohio).

In December, 1987, hundreds of members of our congregation journeyed to Washington, D.C. to join 100,000 fellow Jews from all over North America to rally for the freedom of Soviet Jews. Year after year at our Seder celebrations we read the special "Matzah of Hope," a prayer for the redemption of our Soviet brothers and sisters. Now, almost with a sense of unreality, we learn of the thousands of Jews leaving the Soviet Union every day. Never in our fondest dreams did we expect that our prayers would be answered so swiftly and so completely.

Only 2½ years ago my wife, Maxine, and I were crowded into a small apartment in Leningrad studying Torah with Jewish couples, young and old, like yourselves, who longed for the privilege of living a free Jewish life. Standing now under the chuppah, with 25 Soviet Jewish couples exchanging marriage vows, such a short time after that experience in Leningrad (and a similar one in Moscow a few days later) is one of the great privileges of my life, and one of the most supreme miracles of modern times. So tonight we celebrate and rejoice, and take justified pride in the part we played in helping the Exodus of 1990 and 1991 come to pass; and in the valiant labors we have put forth to see the reality of this day. We thank Almighty God for making it possible, as we recite together the words of the ancient prayer of thanksgiving:

> *Baruch atah Adonai, Eloheynu melech ha-olam, shehecheyanu, vekimanu, vehigianu la-z'man hazeh.* Blessed are You, Lord our God, Ruler of the Universe, who has kept us in life, and sustained us, and enabled us to reach this unique moment.

As the 50 of you stand in the sanctuary of the Lord, freely committing your lives to each other in accordance with the laws of Moses and the people Israel, you symbolize the millions of Soviet Jews who now are either beginning their new lives of Jewish freedom, or who are about to do so. As I address you, I also address your friends, relatives, neighbors — all your brothers and sisters of the House of Israel, whom God has blessed with the greatest gift which we celebrated just a few weeks ago during the Festival of Pesach: the great gift of freedom and liberation from bondage.

Now you are being married, each couple of the 25 of you, for the second time (except for one couple taking their vows for the first time). The first time you were married in the now-defunct Soviet Union, you did not have the opportunity to stand under the chuppah, or drink the two cups of wine, or sign the ketubah, or break the glass. Now you have another opportunity. It is a new wedding. It is the same as the first one in that your feelings for each other are the same, and even stronger. But it is different because now your relationship is consecrated by God. Jewish tradition tells us: No man without a wife, no woman without a husband, no couple without God. Your relationship now adds the sacred dimension of *kedusha* — of holiness — even as this very ceremony is called in Hebrew *Kiddushin* (sanctification).

Rosh Hodesh: A New Month, A New Life

Today and tonight is a minor festival in the Jewish calendar known as *Rosh Hodesh* — the first day of the new Hebrew month of Iyar, a very special month in Jewish history. Iyar is the month in which our people returned to its homeland 43 years ago, the month in which we celebrate the new Jewish holiday of *Yom Ha'Atzma'ut*, Israel Independence Day. How appropriate it is that this special wedding ceremony is taking place just a few days before the Festival in which we celebrate the return of the Jewish people to the pages of world history.

In synagogues all over the world yesterday, on Shabbat morning, a special prayer was recited for the new month of Iyar: *Birkat Ha-Hodesh*, or *Rosh Hodesh Benschen*. Knowing the precarious nature of human existence, our ancestors included in the worship of Shabbat before a new Hebrew month a special prayer for the safety and welfare of our people during the coming month. It is this prayer, and its beautiful hopes for a month of blessing, a life of blessing, *Chaim shel B'racha*, that I would share with you at this sacred moment of your renewal of wedding vows, in the hope that all its aspirations come true for you. A central line in this prayer for the new month includes the following words:

> May God who wrought miracles for our ancestors, redeeming them from slavery to freedom, redeem us soon and gather our dispersed from the four corners of the earth in the fellowship of the entire people Israel.

Just as God is now fulfilling that line of the prayer, so may God also fulfill for all these couples the remainder of the prayer.

The Rosh Hodesh Blessings

The Rosh Hodesh prayer asks for a month of *b'racha* and *tova* — blessing and goodness. The wedding ceremony, which you just heard chanted by the Cantor, is filled with the word *b'racha*. It is one of the most widely-used and special terms in all of the Hebrew language. We at The Park Synagogue wish for all of you a life of *b'racha* (blessing), of God's blessing for goodness all the days of your life. The prayer asks God for *chiddush* (renewal): that the new month not just be a repetition of the past month, but a period of time filled with new experiences, new occasions for rejoicing, and new opportunities for growth, for learning, for sharing, for coming closer together as a couple and a family.

The Rosh Hodesh prayer also expresses the hope that our lives will be without *busha ukhlima* — without shame and reproach. Your life in the former Soviet Union was not, I am sure, without shame and reproach, because you are Jews. Now, here in the free land of the United States of America, your lives will be free of shame and reproach, and filled with pride and joy in your celebrating your Jewishness. We, the members of this congregation, pledge that you will be taught the beauty, sweetness, rapture, and ecstasy of being Jewish, and that all of your memories of shame and reproach associated with being a Jew will fade farther and farther into the past.

The Rosh Hodesh prayer asks that our lives be filled with *osher ve-kavod* (abundance and honor). You are surely entitled to as much of that as God and your own diligent efforts will bring to you, and as a Jewish community we promise to assist you in any possible way to help you fulfill that dream, even as we have attempted to do so already.

This beautiful prayer which we pray for you this evening also asks that we have *ahavat Torah* and *yirat Shamayim* — love of Torah and reverence for God. These are blessings which you could not have known in your former country. We are proud that these blessings have brought a great deal of richness into our lives, and we want you to experience that richness as well. There are few blessings in life that can bring a couple more closeness, warmth, and spiritual satisfaction, than love of Torah and reverence for God — *ahavat Torah ve-yirat Shamayim*.

Ordinarily when a Jewish wedding is held, and a Jewish couple stands under the chuppah before the rabbi, the family and close friends are invited to join the event. Many of those here tonight are your family and friends. But for some of you who are new to Cleveland, you do not have a large family or a large circle of friends. We, the members of this congregation, want you to consider us both your family, your *mishpocha*, and your friends. We consider it an honor and a privilege to be here tonight sharing this milestone event with you. This great and beautiful sanctuary of God is filled with the members of our congregation and of the Jewish community who have gathered tonight to share God's blessings with you, to rejoice, to laugh, and to cry with you. We are here because we know what being married under the chuppah means to a Jewish couple and a Jewish home. It is among the most wonderful honors and privileges that any person can have.

As the new month of Iyar begins tonight, so may a new chapter in your lives begin, as in the words of the Siddur:

Chaim arukim, chaim shel shalom,
A long life and a peaceful life.

Chaim shel b'racha, chaim shel parnasah,
A life of blessing and a life of sustenance.

Chaim shel osher ve-khavod,
A life of abundance and honor.

Chaim she-tehay vanu ahavat Torah ve-yirat Shamayim,
A life embracing piety and love of Torah.

Chaim she-yimalu mishalot leebaynu le-tova,
A life in which your heart's desires for goodness shall be fulfilled.

Amen, selah!

THE JEWISH PEOPLE'S OUTSTRETCHED ARM
Rescuing Ethiopian Jewry

We Jews know that we are an extraordinary people. We are a family, and when we witness our global family's extraordinary treatment of one another, it is rewarding and reassuring.

I recently returned from a five-day mission to Ethiopia (January, 1991) to inspect the condition of the Jewish community in Addis Ababa. Our trip was organized by the American Rabbinic Network for Ethiopian Jewry (ARNEJ), and I was one of three rabbis on the mission. The most powerful impression this visit left all three of us is that our Jewish family is doing a remarkable job of caring for its needy brothers and sisters. When the ancient Israelites were oppressed by Pharaoh in Egypt, the Torah tells us that God brought them out with a mighty hand and an outstretched arm. The outstretched arm of our people, especially in Israel, has accomplished modern miracles in rescuing and caring for the remnants of the House of Israel.

We arrived on Friday morning, January 11, from Tel Aviv by way of Cairo. Exhausted by the all-night flight, we emerged from the Addis airport tired, unshaven, fearful (I for one had never been in a third-world country before, and only once before in a land ruled by a Marxist government), but full of anticipation. We were met by the local director of the office of the American Association for Ethiopian Jews (AAEJ). Our guide, Glenn Stein, made up our itinerary, and was our driver, teacher, host and friend during the our visit.

ARNEJ and AAEJ work hand in hand to achieve their common goals - the rescue of 23,000 Jews desperately trying to be re-united with their family members in Israel. The two organizations cooperate closely with the Israeli Embassy in Addis Ababa, with the American Joint Distribution Committee, and with the North American Conference on Ethiopian Jewry, all of whom have offices and staff on site working diligently to attend to the needs of our Ethiopian family.

On the way to our hotel we discussed the importance of the work being done by the Jewish community to alleviate the problems of Beta Yisrael (the name the Ethiopian Jews prefer, rather than Falashas, which means "stranger" in Amharic, the local tongue). Our visit was to witness *pidyon sh'vuyim*, the rescue of the captives, as our tradition would call it. A talmudic source calls this the highest mitzvah Judaism mandates.

I wondered what kind of rapport I might have with these Jews, whose language I didn't speak, whose ethnicity drastically differed from mine, as an Ashkenazi Jew. Separated from one another for some 2000 years or more, members of Beta Yisrael knew nothing until this century, of post-biblical Judaism. They use no Hebrew in their worship, require no minyan for worship, do not use tallit in prayer, and know nothing of post-biblical holidays, such as Hanukkah.

Nevertheless it is obvious that these people are devoted Jews. They read the same Sidrah (weekly Torah lesson) we do each Shabbat morning. Their Sabbath day is the center of their week and their life. They maintain a biblical kashrut, observe the pilgrimage festivals (Pesach, Shavuot and Sukkot), and are taught Scripture by rabbis whom they call *kohanim*, or *kessim*. Their synagogue (which they call *mesgid*) is important in their religious lives, and most of all, they long to return to Zion, and be reunited with the Jewish People in its Homeland.

We found few men in their 20's to 40's. Most of them had crossed the border into the Sudan during 1984, and were whisked to Israel during Operation Moses (November, December, 1984). They left behind the elderly, women, children, and the ill, whom they hoped would follow soon through family unification. Most of them are still waiting, six years later. [Only 5 months after our visit Operation Solomon took place on May 24, 1991, the miraculous 24-hour rescue operation by the Israel Government and the Israel Defense Forces, rescuing some 15,000 Jews. Since then almost all Ethiopian Jews have reached Israel].

It did not take long to find a strong bond between us. Glenn arranged for a young Ethiopian Jew who had returned to Addis from Israel, Simcha, to translate for us, and be the go-between in all matters of communication. Sometimes we spoke with words, other times with a handshake or a hug, or a smile, or even a few Hebrew words which they picked up from visiting Israeli teachers over the years. "Shabbat Shalom," "Lehitraot!" or "Todda Rabba" were heard often.

Our first venture out of the hotel, Friday afternoon, was to visit the JDC clinic, where we discovered medical care that was on the level of the finest hospitals in all of Africa. An American Jewish physician, Dr. Ric Hodes, was in charge of this simple but efficient medical facility, with four Ethiopian physicians and several Registered Nurses assisting. The clinic was responsible for medical care, a medical outreach program, through which social workers visited homes to assure regular visits and the taking of medications, a nutrition education program, and a complete system of rehabilitation.

For centuries, the Jewish community lived in the far northern province of Ethiopia called Gondar, where they were farmers, craftspeople and artisans. In June, July and August, 1990, they were told that the road from Gondar to Addis Ababa, which had been closed by Eritrean rebels for some time, was now open, and their best chance of emigration was to take the long and risky trip to the capital city and wait there for an exit visa to Israel.

Recent reports that large numbers of Jews will soon leave were not substantiated by the authorities with whom we met. During November and December, 1990, approximately 500 left each month, and in January about 700. Even if that number were raised to 1000 per month, as is hoped, it will take two years to get them all out. During those two years, it is feared that rains, harsh winter weather, robbery, and inability to cope with the exigencies of city life, will decimate their population. We did not leave with great hope that these Jews will be saved quickly enough.

Friday night we were invited to a home of one of the 40 Israelis who serve in one capacity or another in Addis, for the Israeli Embassy or one of the relief organizations. Sitting with this group of dedicated people, we found them to be true heroes to the Beta Yisrael community. We learned that AAEJ began a number of labor-intensive cottage industries to keep the people occupied productively and meaningfully, and help them earn a few extra dollars for daily subsistence. The women weave beautiful baskets of different sizes and shapes, which are sold in the U.S. Others make farm implements and sell them, and still others recycle into mattresses the burlap bags in which their wheat allocations arrive.

On Shabbat morning we worshipped with the thirty kessim (rabbis) of the community on the grounds of the Israeli Embassy. The service was held in Ge'ez, the ancient Ethiopian religious language, and no prayer books were used. We did not understand any of the words, yet now and then we could pick up something like "God of Abraham, God of Isaac, God of Jacob," or "Sh'ma Yisrael," and we knew we were with our own family. At the end of the service we held a discussion with the kessim (through our interpreter, Simcha), sharing some of the differences in our worship, in both style and content, and mostly conveyed the message that we were there to help, to learn, to assure these leaders that they and their people were not forgotten. We closed our visit by singing to them the Israeli song composed for the words of Chasidic Rabbi Nachman of Bratslav — "The whole world is a narrow bridge, but the most important thing is not to be afraid."

Looking out our hotel window, we peered down to the street below where simple shacks dotted the landscape. We were sitting in a luxurious Hilton Hotel in the midst of grinding, abject poverty, where the average income of an Ethiopian family is about $100 per annum, and where no major natural resources, little important industry or economic development can be found. Shabbat afternoon we took a long walk through the suburb of Shola, where 80% of the Jews live, to see with our own eyes the conditions under which they survive. It was beyond belief. Their "homes" were the size of an American bathroom, as primitive as one can be, lacking electricity, heat, light, and plumbing. Their food was provided both by distribution of healthy rations from the JDC, and from a monthly allowance from the Israeli Embassy. No one starved, or lacked medical care. But even their tukuls (bamboo tents) in Gondar were more comfortable than these mud shacks.

Sunday was filled with a series of high-level briefings by the Israeli ambassador,

Asher Naim, by the Israeli officials at the Jewish Agency, the Israeli JDC, and the American Association for Ethiopian Jewry. We also had occasion to meet with some 15 Ethiopian Israelis who had returned to their native land to assist their families in the process of adjustment and emigration.

Monday was our last full day, and we used the time to revisit the JDC clinic during normal operating hours and to examine the exciting educational program on the grounds of the Israeli Embassy in which 4000 children study Hebrew, Jewish culture, their own Amharic language and Ethiopian Jewish history. Little children approached us and stammered in Hebrew to show us how much they had learned, and to establish contact with their visitors from far away. They are deeply attached and grateful to Jews who come from Israel, Europe, and the US, who help them realize their dream to journey to the Land of Israel.

In the afternoon we had a long visit with the American Chargé D'Affairs, Robert Hodek, who was extremely gracious in sharing with us his own assessment of the Jewish situation. We expressed our gratitude to the American authorities for the wonderful assistance and cooperation they have offered to our people in their slow and painful struggle to cope with a very difficult situation.

By the end of our visit, we were extremely proud of what the "long, outstretched arm" of the Jewish people and our agencies are accomplishing, working under extremely adverse conditions. Knowing that most blacks in the U.S. and elsewhere left Africa in slave ships, mistreated by Western mercantilists (including American colonists), who starved, flogged and whipped them, it was very inspiring to see the selfless devotion of dozens of Jews from Israel, Europe and the U.S., who were serving, Schweitzer-like, to ease the lot of our suffering family members, and assist them in their life-long dream of returning to Zion.

To make sure that everything is done to speed up the emigration of the remnants of Ethiopian Jewry, write our President and government leaders to continue to press for their release. Write and encourage our Israeli co-workers, and congratulate them on the wonderful and extraordinary mitzvot they are performing. Send your contributions to the American Rabbinic Network for Ethiopian Jewry (859 S. Oakland Avenue, Pasadena, CA 91106).

With all the problems and burdens facing world Jewry today, it is difficult to know which of the many worthwhile causes we should support. The redemption of these beautiful People of the Book should rank right up there near the top of the list.

[How grateful we can be that, as of this writing, Spring, 1993, Beta Yisrael is safely transported to Israel. Their needs for housing, jobs, learning Hebrew, and social integration, however, continue unabated. The work continues].

TIME TO SPEAK UP FOR JONATHAN POLLARD

On December 21, 1985, Jonathan Jay Pollard, a 31-year-old civilian counter-intelligence analyst for the US Navy, was arrested for spying. His wife Anne was arrested as an accomplice. Pollard confessed that he had spied for Israel, and cooperated with the government in preparing his case. On June 6, 1986, he and Anne pleaded guilty through a plea-bargaining arrangement. No trial was held. On March 4, 1987, Judge Aubrey Robinson, of the US District Court in Washington, DC, sentenced Jonathan to life imprisonment and Anne to two concurrent 5-year terms.

The American Jewish community has been outraged (though silently) about the sentence. Pollard's lawyer, Prof. Alan J. Dershowitz of the Harvard Law School, questions the appropriateness of the life sentence for someone spying for an ally. In another case, Samuel Morrison, a Navy intelligence analyst who sold classified photos to a magazine, did not cooperate with the government and did not plead guilty, yet he was sentenced to only 2 years in prison and was released after 8 months. However, Pollard's sentence is similar to those given John Walker and Ronald Pelton, who both spied for years for (our then enemy) the Soviet Union.

The Pollard spy case has been an embarrassment to US Jewry. American Jews were angry that Israel would use an American Jew as a spy, and thus give new life to the nasty canard of dual loyalty. We Jews have a right as Americans and human beings to challenge injustice, even in such a case. Let's look at the crime, sentence, conditions of imprisonment, and the reactions of American Jewry.

The Crime

In 1979, Jonathan Pollard began to work in Navy Intelligence. He reported that in his Navy unit he ran into verbal anti-Semitism. More importantly, despite directives to transmit documents to Israel, according to the "American-Israel Exchange Information Agreement" signed by Ronald Reagan in 1983, lower level officials refused to comply.

In 1984, five years after Pollard began to work for the Navy, and 1½ years before his arrest, he began to transmit thousands of documents to Israel -- 360 cubit feet of information. Driven by a passionate ideological commitment to Israel and a deep concern about Israel's security, he transmitted what he thought Israel deserved legally. But Pollard did not take his naval job in order to spy! At first, he was not paid for the documents he provided Israel; later, however, he did accept a modest amount, and was sucked into a pattern. At his sentencing, Pollard admitted, "I should be punished; I broke the law." Few deny that, or condone his behavior, besides followers of Meir Kahane.

Events of the Gulf War shed new light on both the value and motivation of Jonathan Pollard's actions. The majority of the information transmitted related to precise US-gathered information about Iraqi chemical warfare production capabilities, including detailed satellite pictures and maps showing the location of factories and storage facilities. Pollard questioned his superiors about why this information was being withheld from Israel. One of them, Pollard says, "turned to me laughing and said that the Jews were overly sensitive about gas due to their experiences during the Second World War and should just calm down a bit."

The U.S. did not want Israel to have this information for fear that Israel might make a preemptive strike. Had Pollard not informed Israel of Iraq's chemical threat, Israel would not have had confidence in its preparedness for a potentially deadly disaster and would not have been able to exercise the extraordinary self-restraint it showed during the Gulf War in January, 1991.

The Sentence

The plea-bargain arrangement meant that Pollard was not to be charged with treason, and was to be indicted only on one count: giving information to an ally. For his cooperation in providing information to the Government, which led to the indictment of four Israelis, the Government promised not to seek a life sentence. In Pollard's motion this year to vacate his plea of guilty and have a trial, he states that the government made three promises: 1) not to seek a life sentence, 2) to limit statements it made to the court about the sentence to the facts and circumstances of the offenses committed, and 3) it promised to inform the court of Pollard's cooperation and of the considerable value of the cooperation. The government reneged on all three promises.

A life sentence is extraordinarily harsh for a person spying on an ally. Why was Pollard sentenced so mercilessly and unjustly?

1. One can only speculate that in his role in the Pollard case, Caspar Weinberger, then Secretary of Defense, was trying to prove to the world that he not only is not Jewish, but is anti-Zionist. Weinberger sent a secret memo to Judge Aubrey Robinson the day before sentencing. We have an idea of what the memo said judging from the comments Weinberger made on another occasion: "The Pollard case was the worst case of spying in U.S. history," and that "the Pollards deserve to be shot."

   Can Secretary Weinberger be serious when he said that, "It is difficult for me to conceive of a greater harm to national security than that caused by Mr. Pollard?" What about the Walker family, who, before Glasnost, gave Russia our military codes and CIA connections behind the Iron Curtain?

What about the Iran-Contra affair, in which our enemy, Iran was given arms and ammunition that might still be fired on American ships or troops? Can we compare these incidents to giving information to an ally — for which not one American could possibly be killed?

2. The actions of Judge Aubrey Robinson are also vital to the case. Robinson is said to have compared Israelis to Nazis, and promised to "teach Israel a lesson about American justice." Judge Robinson, an African-American, was aware of Pollard's role in transmitting information to Israel regarding Israeli-South African relations. In an affidavit to the appeal, Pollard's attorney, Alan Dershowitz, states that he felt that "the Pollard-South Africa connection had weighed heavily in [Robinson's] decision to impose a life sentence. . . ."

We know that Caspar Weinberger has a visceral hatred of Israel and the special place it holds in American foreign policy. Since the severe sentence seems to be largely due to his secret memo to Judge Robinson, it is likely that Robinson also bears similar feelings towards Israel and any American Jews who would violate American law for its welfare.

Conditions of Imprisonment

During the first year of his imprisonment, Pollard was in Springfield, Missouri in a prison ward for the criminally insane, where psychotics are held. He was told by the Government that he would stay there as long as he didn't given them the names of the other American Jews who collaborated with him, and was specifically asked about such distinguished American Jewish leaders as Morris Abram and Howard Squadron. Pollard denied any connection with these men. After Representative Lee Hamilton of Indiana protested to the Justice Department, Pollard was moved to a federal prison in Marion, Illinois, where he remains.

Since moving to Marion, Pollard spends much of his time in solitary confinement, supposedly to protect him from anti-Semitic groups such as the Aryan Brotherhood. In a hand-written letter to me (and, I am sure, in similar ones to many of my colleagues), Pollard asked me to acknowledge receipt of his letter, "given the problems I've experienced with my mail." Visitation and phone privileges are highly restricted. Meanwhile, Anne Pollard, who suffered from a serious intestinal disease, was denied medication and treatment and lost 60 pounds before her five year sentence was recently completed.

American Jewish Reaction

During the last few months some leading voices in American Jewish leadership have begun to support Pollard. Resolutions from many Jewish organizations are demanding that the case be re-opened.

In the early days of the Pollard episode, the Israeli scholar Shlomo Avineri wrote in the Jerusalem Post that American Jews were suffering from a Galut mentality. In a review of the new Dershowitz book, *Chutzpah*, Sidney Zion quotes Dershowitz: "Despite our apparent success, deep down we see ourselves as second-class citizens — as guests in another people's land." Zion comments: "I think most Jews . . . feel the country really belongs to the goyim, that uneasy lies the head that wears even an invisible yarmulke." Embarrassed by the Pollard affair, we have maintained silence, hoping that no one would accuse us of being disloyal citizens.

American Jews, American Jewish organizations, the Jewish intellectual community, synagogues, and rabbis have all remained silent for too long in the face of this blatant act of injustice. It's time to break the silence, to stand up and be counted.

WHY SOCIAL JUSTICE IS A THING OF THE FUTURE
Notes for a Lecture

I TRADITIONAL JEWISH MOTIVATIONS FOR SOCIAL JUSTICE

1) **Jewish Ethics:**
   Torah: You shall not mistreat the stranger, the oppresssed, the downtrodden, the widow, the orphan, the hungry.

2) **Jewish History:**

   a) Historical experience.

   b) Tradition of persecution, discrimination, prejudice; heightened sensitivity. "Out of my flesh I know" (Job)

   c) Jewish value concepts *(Kadushin)*: Zedek, mishpat, shalom, shalom bayit, kibbud av va-em, kedushat Ha-chayyim, kevod habriyot, rachmanim b'nai rachmanim, yetziyat mitzrayim, tzorchay zibbur, or la-goyim, kol yisrael arevim ze lazeh, musar, gemilut hasadim, ahavat yisrael, tzaar baalay chayim.

   d) Jewish Liturgy
   Sacralization, mythification, ritualization, symbolization, of value concepts & ideas referred to above.

   e) Specific Jewish role in world history - counter culture (subset of *or la-goyim*). Midrash: *Ivri* means whole world on one side, Avraham on other side (thus called "Avraham Ha-Ivri").

II CONTEMPORARY FORCES THAT CREATE NEW LEVELS OF READINESS FOR RENEWED SOCIAL JUSTICE ACTIVISM

1) **Our shrinking globe.**

   Heightened sensitivity to people far away; interconnectedness of humanity; more rapid awareness of problems (took US 3 days to find out Lincoln was assassinated - JFK, almost within minutes whole world knew); increased effect on one another because of heightened technology.

   a) Marshall McLuhan's term: global village, more & more a reality thru communications technology (satellites, rapid transportation, super-sonic airplanes, Reagen's promise of sub-orbital flights - 3 hrs to China, sub-oceanic cables, fax machines, etc.). TV evening news began Sept. 1963. Seems like it's been around forever. Nov. '63 JFK's assassination & funeral followed by whole world. Some years later, in Carter administration, each night # days American hostages taken counted on TV, drove Carter out of office. Vietnam war watched daily on TV - watched butchery, carnage - changed perception of war - now participating, not sending boys "overseas."

Watching oppression in S. Africa - changes world opinion, when see blacks hit by clubs, treated like animals.

Intifada would never have turned tide of world opinion against Israel had it not been for TV, watching Israelis on eve news clubbing little Palestinian children, but not seeing them throw their Molotov cocktails.

b) Chernobyl - example. Not only drinking water in Kiev, but milk in Finland, air in Kansas City,

c) Talmudic story - 2 men in boat, one wants to cut hole his side. Other - what you do affects me!

d) Golden Rule - Love your neighbor as yourself! (Rabbi Akiva: *ze klal gadol baTorah* - This is a great Principle in the Torah). Who is neighbor today? We discovered that child in Chernobyl is our neighbor, mother in Helsinki, babies in Ethiopia). New definition of neighbor. In global village all are neighbors.

e) Cain & Abel story - today every murder is fratricide.

2) **Dangers have escalated - proportionately enlarged, increased by geometric proportions.**

   a) Nuclear warfare
   George Bush wanted to appoint man as Secretary of Defense, 2nd in line to push nuclear button, who was known alcoholic & highly questionable personal moral standards. Nuclear proliferation. Dozens of nations now have bomb. Even while U.S. and Russia reducing arsenals, nuclear technology is being sold throughout the world, and smaller nations are developing their capabilities. Unstable dictators will soon have nuclear potential.

   b) Chemical warfare
   Iran, Iraq, Egypt, Germany, Libya - not to speak of superpowers. Every little jerk-ruler, peanut-brained dictator, can spread life-threatening chemicals that can unleash mass human destruction.

c) Environment
Globe increasingly threatened by abuse of environment, acid rain, depletion of ozone layer, greenhouse effect, raping of world by greedy moguls of industry. Every day news media tell us more foods we shouldn't eat; can't breathe the air; what's left?

d) Drugs
2 million Americans hooked on cocaine, heroin or crack. Old abuses: alcohol, nicotine still powerful detriments to healthy society.

e) Health consciousness
Diseases often come from our own neglect in diet, nutrition, exercise. Jews esp., founders of connection of health to holiness - particularly guilty of ignoring new information and fostering diets hi in cholestoral, saturated fats, high calories, salt. Jewish organizations still serve junk food at teacher-training conferences, Federation meetings, synagogue onegai Shabbat, etc.

AIDS - tremendous needs outstripping ability to help. Needs for hospitals, hospices, home care. Also: new viral diseases we don't yet know about....

3) **New Spiritual Consciousness**

New Age. Heightened awareness of importance of spirituality. (Ex: my new book, rev. ed. of *Glad To Be Me: building Self-Esteem in Yourself and Others*, 3 new chapters, on self-esteem & women, handicapped, spirituality).

a) New consciousness means new awareness of problems of self, others, relationships, family, society, unity of globe. Ideas of "New Age", Book of Miracles. New interest in Mysticism - unity of human species.

b) In religious terms: one world. End of <u>alenu</u> prayer: - "on that day the Lord shall be one and God's name <u>one</u>." Many other texts: Shma: *Hashem echad* - "The Lord is <u>One</u>." Spiritual awakening taking place. Old texts are layered with new meaning: "my brother's keeper." Malachi: "Have we not all one Father?, Hath not one God created us?" Amos: "Are you not, O Children of Israel, like children of Ethiopians to Me?"

As a kid I lived in neighborhood of N. Phila. called Logan, where there were many Orthodox Jews and Orthodox synagogues. Orthodox Jews, they used to say, believed in 3 things: fatherhood of Gd, brotherhood of man, and neighborhood of Logan. This old joke is now more and more true - our unity is becoming clearer and clearer. The world is a small neighborhood.

c) Recent dissolution of many regional conflicts. East-West (Reagen-Gorbachev revolution, from Evil Empire to active cooperation, reduction of arms, etc.). Other exs.: Afghan war, Iran-Iraq War, Warsaw Solidarity, Whales - US & Russia cooperated in saving; Armenian earthquake (even Israel sent help to USSR).

d) Revision in liturgy in Conservative, Reform, & Reconstructionist movements:

Some examples:

Sim shalom ba-olam
al kol yoshvay tayval
Modeh (Modah) ani
she-asani ben (bat) horin, be-tzalmo (Birkot ha-shachar)

e) Flood of consciousness-raising books
Aquarian Conspiracy, by Marilyn Ferguson; *Feminine Mystique*, by Betty Friedan; *Diet for a Small Planet*, by Frances Moore Lappe; *Silent Spring*, by Rachel Carson; *The American Way of Death*, by Jessica Mitford; *The Other America*, by Michael Harrington; several books by John Gardner, founder of Common Cause, Scott Peck's books, *Road Less Travelled, A Different Drummer*; Gerald Jampolsky, Ram Dass; holistic health movement connecting mind, body, and planet; feminist movement and men's movement seeking balance of polarities.

f) Reconstructionist emphasis on community - organic community, ideas of Rabbi Mordecai M. Kaplan - now accepted by all movements. Klal Yisrael - Yitz Greenberg's group called CLAL. From Reconstructionist to Orthodox - the Hebrew term Klal Yisrael (the totality of the Jewish People) has taken on new meaning in the modern age.

Havurah movement - Arthur Green (Havurat Shalom), Harold Schulweis turned it into a synagogue-based movement. Created new generation of community-conscious people, called the "*Jewish Catalogue* generation."

4) **Humanistic & Existential Psychology - Third Force**

a) Abraham Maslow: self-actualization -- highest level of human fulfillment is seeking after truth, justice, wholenss, unity, integrity (Hierarchy of Needs).

b) Erik Erikson: concept of generativity. Erikson divided the life cycle into 8 psychosexual developmental stages -- as we get older, what keeps us alive is our ability to serve others. Either become committed to helping the next generation, and attailn a sense of accomplishment & integration, or stagnate, leading to despair and isolation. Popularization of this idea in JFK inaugural: Ask not what your country can do for you, ask rather what you can do for your country. President Clinton now designing volunteer and service programs modelled on the Kennedy idea.

c) Viktor Frankl - logotherapy. *Man's Search for Meaning*: what sustained him under pressure was **love** - remembering, feeling, love for wife, hers for him. Human love & meaning & purpose in life as indispensable sustaining life forces in human psychology.

d) Gerald Jampolsky - MD, healing, children's cancer center. Books: *Teach Only Love, Love Is Letting Go Of Fear, Out Of Darkness Comes Light*. Main idea: helping others is essence of healing self. Bernie Siegel's books - same idea.

e) George Bernard Shaw:
"This is the true joy in life, the being used for a purpose recognized by yourself as a mighty one; the beilng a force of nature instead of a feverish, selfish little clod of ailments and grievances complaining that the world will not devote itself to making you happy.

"I am of the opinion that my life belongs to the whole community, and as long as I live it is my privilege to do for it whatever I can.

"I want to be thoroughly used up when I die, for the harder I work the more I live. I rejoice in life for its own sake. Life is no "brief candle" to me. It is a sort of splendid torch which I have got hold of for the moment, and I want to make it burn as brightly as possible before handing it on to future generations."

f) Ram Dass (Jewish boy from Boston: Richard Albert) - book on service. New age, meditation crowd, moving focus from self (Me-Decade) to others. Polster, Daniel Yankelovitch: commitment is word for 80's. "New Rules."

5) **Humanistic Education - corollary, spinoff from Humanistic Psychology.**

a) John Dewey - learn from experience, by doing. *Mitzvot maasiyot* (action as religious commandments). Behavioral component in all goals of education. *Mitzvot & Maasim tovim* (performance of mitzvot & good deeds, essential talmudic principles). Not dry academic learning. Kids out in community, service. Action commitment vital part of learning.

(Ex: my son taught Hebrew High School in Boston suburb, where the class studied Jewish tradition on the needs/rights of handicapped; the class built a ramp for the synagogue).

Old Jewish debate in Talmud - which is more important, study or deeds - *midrash o maaseh*? Rabbis answered: *midrash - mipnay she-midrash mayveeh leeday maaseh. Study is more important because it leads to good deeds!*

Many other similar texts: Am Yisrael at Har Sinai: *Naaseh ve-nishma* - do, then understand.

Story: There were two *NY Times* reporters at an Israel Bonds banquet; one Jewish, one non-Jew. At the end of the banquet, the non-Jew turns to the Jew: all night they used the word tachlis , what does it mean? Means: talk less!

Hasidic revolution in Jewish life was action, experience-oriented; human-centered. *Mitnaged loves Shulkhan Arukh*, Hasid loves person who loves Shulkhan Arukh.

Education today relates less to transmission of facts than to changing of people. Rabbi A. J. Heschel said: We need not only text books, but text people!

    b) emphasizes personal growth, values clarification, heightened sensitivity to others; importance of quality of relationships. 3 R's today: Rejoicing, renewing, relating.

6) Influence of Other Traditions

    a) Catholicism in North & South America is a very strong advocate of social justice today. Ex: Liberation Theology; American Bishops' declarations on economic justice, nuclear warfare, etc. Modern secular leftist Jews have "Catholic envy." - Story of the late Paul Cowan (his book *Orphan in History*, Doubleday, 1982, pp. 138-143). In jail with Father Dan Berrigan. Priest turned to him in jail and said: "I'm in here because of Jesus Christ, why are you in here?" Cowan says that this experience pushed him back into Jewishly-rooted social action.

    b) Autobiography of Michael Harrington (*The Other America*, famous

socialist), *The Long-Distance Runner* (Holt, 1988) - reviewed in *NY Times Book Review* (3-16-89, pp. 29-31). Reviewer, Michael Kazin, writes:
"For Harrington this struggle is spiritual and religious as well as political, thus placing him in a little-known tradition of the American left. When jailed for opposing US involvement in WWI, Eugene Debs kept in his cell a single picture - of Christ. Much of Norman Thomas's radical faith came out of his early years as a Prebyterian minister committed to the social gospel. Harrington may have lost his own faith, but he still calls himself a 'pious apostate,' an 'atheist... fellow traveler of moderate Catholicism.'" Reviewer continues by describing the paradox of this atheist-socialist who is at heart a deeply religious man with profound faith that drives his liberal socialism.

c) American tradition of non-violence (from Ghandi).
Martin Luther King, Jr., Civil Rights movement; Rabbi Heschel; American transcendentalist movement - Emerson & Thoreau. When Thoreau in jail because he refused to pay taxes, becoming the first practitioner of "civil disobedience," Emerson said to him: "Henry, what are you doing in there?" Thoreau replied, "Ralph, what are you doing out there?" We have to always ask ourselves: What are we doing out here? Why aren't we <u>in there</u> (figuratively or literally)?

d) Feminism
Contemporary Judaism, women's rights advanced enormously, mainly under influence of women's movement. Women now counted in minyan, given aliyot, ordained as rabbis, cantors; worship - liturgy made more inclusive instead of exclusive - slowly but surely. The Conservative Movement's Committee on Jewish Law and Standards (CJLS) now has a woman - 1st woman ordained as a Conservative rabbi: Amy Eilberg. She's written a teshuva (legal responsum) on the question of special new rituals for miscarriage. If you remember the fact that the people who made halacha for 2000 years were men, you will understand the need for change.

7) **It works!**

We have enough accumulated evidence that democracy, social protest, the will of the people, ultimately emerges triumphant.

a) Exs: Vietnam War; civil rights movement; Soviet Jewry movement (Sharansky: because of housewives & students he was freed). The 90's can learn much from the 60's and 70's. The nineties can be a time of even greater change than the sixties. Ram Dass said: "If you liked the

60's, you'll love the 90's." Other exs.: "Who Is A Jew?" question was tabled in Knesset because of American Jewry. Truth will rise & win.

b) During my USSR trip (Oct, 1988), I visited Edward & Nina Nadgorny - whose son Boris was a student at Princeton U. They told me an incredible story about how Oxford University students invited the Soviet ambassador to London to their campus and asked them why Boris could not leave. The ambassador said "There is no problem, he can leave." The students had a phone hook-up with Moscow, and asked the ambassador to tell Boris directly. After that, there was no way the USSR wouldn't let Boris out - it would have been in the next day's headlines: "Ambassador Lies." All because of determined, clever students at Oxford University, Boris was able to be free, studying at Princeton.

c) After the Yom Kippur War, Oct '73, a popular song emerged in Israel: *Ani ve-ata neshaneh et ha-olam. (You and I can change the world).*

d) Dramatic example of the work of one person.
An angry Michigan mother, Terry Rakolta, annoyed by TV program, "Married . . . With Children" - which she said displayed blatant exploitation of women, sex and anti-family attitudes. Rakolta started a one-person campaign, writing letters to commercial sponsors of the TV program. One by one companies withdrew advertising, incl. Johnson & Johnson, Proctor & Gamble, McDonald's, and Coca Cola Co., from whose president she received an apologetic letter saying he was "corporately professionally and personally embarrassed" that a Coke ad had appeared on such a program.

8) **Reagan-Bush Heritage**

12 years of Reagen-Bush presidencies left an enormous gap in social development of society. Social values losing ground for 12 years - areas such as poverty, hunger, civil rights, affirmative action, abortion rights, government corruption, separation of church & state, environment, education, day care, mental health care, homeless (Reagan: "They like it in the streets.", or "Blacks agitate for selfish reasons, no real justification," - etc. etc.

There used to be a joke about the 3 biggest lies in history: something like: the check is in the mail; some of my best friends are Jews; we now have a new one - George Bush will create a "kinder, gentler nation."

9) **Waning of Volunteerism**

Volunteerism shrinking because of: a) women in working force, b) economy demands two-working parents, c) VCRs, d) When George Bush asks for 1000 points of light, you know we're in deep trouble!

II SOME AREAS OF ACTION NEEDS

A Jewish

1) **Israel**

   a) protect Israel from media, US leaders duped by PLO, danger of drastic & over-accelerated reduction in US Aid for Israel - by Congress

   b) Voice differences between American Jewry & Israel (Who is a Jew?); reluctance to negotiate, give up any land, etc.

2) **Russian Jewry**

   a) visits by rabbis, educators, teachers very important. - The Hebrew speakers, leaders, cultural devotees - mostly leaving....

   b) Advocacy Movement has changed its focus from emigration to: emigration and education (for those staying). From "Let my people go" to "Let my people know." While Jews remain, there is a great need to develop intense Jewish life within former USSR.

   c) Persuade Russian Jews to go to Israel. When they come to US they get lost, assimilate; trade one Diaspora for another.

3) **Ethiopian Jewry**

   50,000 now in Israel. Conditions difficult: Poverty, hunger. Other oppressed Jewish communities: Syria (leaving gradually), Iraq, Iran.

4) **Black-Jewish Relations**

   Desparate need for reconciliation, end polarization, restore early coalition. So much can be accomplished for us and for America, if we work together.

5) **Interfaith**

   Jewish-Christian-Moslem (Salman Rushdie, *Satanic Verses*). Not all Moslems are fundamentalists - need to avoid stereotypes, form new alliances with American Moslems of good will.

6) **Church-State separation**

   Prayer in public schools. Creche & Hanukkah menorahs (Chabad). Supreme Court Justice Sandra Day O'Conner wrote a letter, May 1988, citing cases for Arizona legislature that America is a Christian country.

7) **Anti-Semitism**

   New ADL study, 20% rise since Intifada. Skinheads. Neo-Nazism, here and in Germany.

8) **Synagogue Mitzvah Corps**

   Also called: Sunshine Committee, para-rabbinics, Caring Community, etc. Visit hospitals, nursing homes, shiva calls, hospice, help divorcing families, homebound, rides to events.

9) **Nutrition at Jewish meetings**

   People who first made connection between food and physical/spiritual health - kashrut - today among biggest offenders in good eating habits. Jewish diets high in cholesterol, sugar, calories, saturated fats. Federation & other agencies: cold cuts, cake at Oneg Shabbat, - coffee & Danish or donuts, rarely piece of fruit available.

10) **Male-female sex roles**

    Liturgy - utilize rights women have won - aliyot, talit & tefillin, minyan, kippah. Gender-sensitive liturgy.

    Arthur Waskow: androgynist transformation of Judaism - whole new era of Judaism, new stage of spiritual growth & transformation.

11) **Jewish Education**

    Promote profession, thru local & national advocacy organizations, such as CAJE. Power in numbers. Raise standards of profession. Song of Songs: *Et karmi lo natarti* "My own vineyard I have neglected." Higher salaries, more prestige, full time positions, benefits, recognition.

B) **General/Secular**

1) **Nuclear proliferation**

   Join Shalom Center in Philadelphia, led by Arthur Waskow. Fight for nuclear freeze. Waskow : Once upon a time, the *Shalosh Regalim* - the three "foot-march" festivals - were really marches, rallies, demonstrations. Hundreds of thousands of people came to Jerusalem in a massive demonstratlion not only of religious devotion but of political power - the power of numbers. But in the Diaspora, we have celebrated these festivals - eaten at our Sedarim, built our Sukkot - in our scattered homes and synagogues, in the nooks and crannies of the societies around us, not en masse. What would it mean now for us to gather again in thousands at Pesach to oppose the Pharaohs who threaten to drown in Floods of Fire not only the boy-babies of our own people, but all the children of all the peoples? What would it mean to gather again in thousands , before the White House, the Soviet Embassy, a nuclear missile base - to build and live in the Sukkot Shalom that are the open, vulnerable, leafy, light-filled inverse of a fallout shelter?" ("Tikkun Olam," *CCAR Yearbook*, Vol 94, 1984, pp. 22-23).

2) **Ecology**

Report issued by Congress - Rep. Henry Waxman - an observant, commited Jew from Southern Calif.: in 1987 more than 2.4 billion lbs. of toxic waste contaminants were released, mostly by chemical companies, on USA. About 10 lbs. for every man, woman, child in USA. Waxman: "The magnitude of this problem far exceeds our worst fears." Among 320 chemicals included iln the survey by the EPA were 60 carcinogens. Of these 60 cancer-causing chemicals, U.S. Public Health Services lists, it regulataes only 7.

Simply put: we need a new Clean Air Bill, and we have to push Congrss to do it. Also need to force polluting companies and industries to stop: Chemical companies, dry cleaners, metals, rubbers, plastics, and automobiles - all release toxic contaminants. Only other alternative: move to Hawaii or Nevada, 2 cleanest states in US.

Growing literature on ecology. See Vice-President Al Gore's wonderful book, *Earth in the Balance - Ecology and the Human Spirit*. Join the new Jewish organization for ecology: Shomray Adamah (Keepers of the Earth). They have a catalog of wonderful publications.

3) **Animal rights**

Jews have history of sensitivity to animals. Rabbinic concept of *Tzaar Baalay Chaim* (prohibition on causing pain to animals). Do our kids know that phrase? Know about the role that sensitivity to animals plays in kashrut? Wearing of fur - hats, coats, leather shoes.... Issues to discuss, debate, - bring to bear traditional Jewish sources.

4) **Government ethics/accountability**

PACS, honoraria for Congresspersons; ethics legislations (which Reagen vetoed). In Reagen-Bush administrations government ethics is an oxymoron.

Join: Common Cause, Public Citizen - or similar organizations.

5) **AIDS**

Gay rights. I visited San Francisco last December. Out to dinner with colleague, Rabbi Ted Alexander. Asked gays "Why need own synagogues?" - They gave two answers : a) couple wants an aliyah on their "anniversary" - they can't, b) the synagogues hold socials and they can't dance together. Many others. More understanding in Jewish community needed. We need to fight gay-bashing, and do much more to protect gay rights, to facilitate greater equality for gays/lesbians. There is increasing evidence that being gay is genetic, and if people have no control over their sexual orienttion, we need to understand and treat them differently.

6) **Substance abuse**

Alcohol, drugs, nicotine, caffein - all problems which in the past were not ours, but are today in the Jewish community as well - big denial goes on. Synagogues need to sponsor AA & other twelve-step groups, not force Jews to go to churches.

7) **Women's issues**

Male-female sex roles: battered wives, child advocacy, child abuse, child care, Jewish family life education.

8) **Handicapped**

Jewish & other communal buildings. ORT published a book on handicap accessibility.

9) **Illiteracy**

10) **Abortion**

Pro-choice. Roe vs. Wade will be chipped away, until back to coat-hanger abortions for poor, and doctors offices for rich, or travel to far places. With Clinton administration things are changing, but the President needs support in the grass roots.

11) Homeless

The Liberty Bell in Phila. has a biblical quotation: -"Proclaim Liberty Throughout the Land, to all the inhabitants thereof." - Liberty in Hebrew is dror. Medieval commentator Rashi explains: the roots dar and dur are the same, freedom is related etymologically to living - liberty means have a place to live, freedom to live wherever you can afford.

12) Hunger

We must support the international Jewish organization called Mazon: the Jewish Response to Hunger. The plan is to have everyone holding a simcha contribute 3% of the cost to Mazon.

13) Business Ethics

(Boesky, Wall St.; study Jewish sources; produce texts books on Jewish business ethics for all ages. Moral education - Kohlberg, Values Clarification; Melton Center. Need to teach ethics in Jewish schools.

14) Medical Ethics

Euthanasia; genetic engineering; human experimentation; living wills; organ transplants & organ donations (sign driver's license?)

15) Wellness

Nutrition - labeling; education, exercise. The verse in Deuteronomy says: *Ve-nishmartem m'od le-nafshotaychem.* (Take care of your body, your health). Tradition of mind-body-spirit connection in Judaism is strong and ancient. Cf. books: *Healing and the Mind* by Bill Moyers, (Doubleday, 1993); *Mind Body Medicine - How To Use Your Mind For Better Health,* ed. Daniel Goleman & Joel Gurin, Consumer Reports Books. Where is the Jewish book on wellness, the mind-body-health connection?

16) Human Rights

S. Africa, China, Iran, Syria. Cf. source: Action Plan of NJCRAC.

IV - EDUCATIONAL STRATEGIES

1) **Talmud Torah**

   Cognitive, text study. Sacred texts. Value concepts.

   Sample Bible texts: Genesis 1, Leviticus 19, Psalm 24, Isaiah 58 (Yom Kippur Haftara), Job 28, Jonah. Siddur texts: *alenu*; *al chet*; *Mishna Peah* from early morning service; Sanhedrin Mishna 4:5; musar literature - *middot*.

2) **Values Clarification, values realization**

   Clarifying Jewish Values, Jewish Consciousness Raising, by Dov Peretz Elkins.

3) **Moral Education**

   Continual research & publication on theories of moral education founded by Lawrence Kohlberg of Harvard. Cf. writings of Dr. Jerry Friedman of Los Angeles.

4) *Mitzvot Maasiyot*

   Community projects - for milestones, such as Bar/bat Mitzvah, Confirmation, Hebrew High graduation; letter writing campaigns. Zedakah Councils - Danny Siegel books on private Zedakah (Ziv Zedakah Funds) - personal selections. Projects for hungry, homeless; collection and delivery of holiday baskets to Jewish elderly/needy families.

5) **Demonstrations**

   Local, regional, national

6) **Trips**

   Russia (USY) - Israel, Europe - Holocaust sites. Local Holocaust Museums (Washington, Los Angeles). Ellis Island. Institute of Leadership and Values in Washington, D.C. led by Rabbi Sidney Schwartz, is an extraordinary experience.

7) **Awareness**

   Advocacy speakers, films, videos, tapes, etc.

8) **Simulation games**

Federation budget allocation; Rambam's 8 steps; Gestapo; Soviet Jewry emigration. Cf. *Experiential Programs for Jewish Groups, The Ideal Jew,* and *Why Did Susan Cohen Desert Judaism?* published by Growth Associates, 212 Stuart Rd. East, Princeton, NJ 08540.

9) **Experiential learning**

Bernard Reisman (*The Experiential Book*), and experiential series by Dov Peretz Elkins.

10) **Visualization**

Image perfect society; what change, what leave, what add, what omit. Imagery and visualization are becoming important educational techniques, and a very large literature is accumulating.

******

PRESCRIPTION FOR A LONG AND HAPPY LIFE
Age-Old Wisdom for the New Age

With wit and insight, Rabbi Dov Peretz Elkins teaches us about the life of the spirit, and the true spirit of life. His book is full of wisdom from sources both ancient and modern.
Rabbi David J. Wolpe, author, The Healer of Shattered Hearts

Only one who believes passionately that there is no substitute for the inspirational, emotional and intellectual stimulation that a well-crafted sermon can bring can produce the kind of sermons found in this volume in such marvelous abundance.... Experienced preachers will find a veritable goldmine of ideas....Rabbis who are just beginning their careers will find in the volume ample proof of the potential effectiveness of a carefully planned and architected sermon. They will accept no substitutes.
Rabbi Sidney Greenberg, Dresher, PA

You will find yourself caught up in Rabbi Elkins' sermons from the first sentence and you will not be able to put them down. He tells stories like a master and preaches with brilliance.
Rabbi Charles Kroloff, Westfield, NJ

Dov Peretz Elkins challenges us to be alert to the richness and beauty of Jewish life. His sermons reflect familiarity with a variety of sources, and are firmly grounded in Jewish values and tradition.
Rabbi Arnold Goodman, Atlanta

Once again Dov Peretz Elkins presents us with a volume of material that combines the keen discernment of humanistic psychology with the timeless insights of Jewish sacred texts. He does this without restorting to technical language or pretentious displays of erudition. His writings are peppered with anecdotes and tales that keep the reader engaged from beginning to end. An invaluable tool for those who seek support in the struggle and insecurities of day-to-day life.
Rabbi Haskell M. Bernat, Long Beach

A marvelous homiletic resource. Rabbi Elkins writes lucidly and trenchantly. He throws light on perennial problems with Jewish and general sources. He is the preacher's preacher.
Rabbi Dr. Abner Weiss, Beverly Hills

Rabbi Dov Peretz Elkins is both a student of Torah's eternal meaning and a compassionate observer of contemporary human struggles. His writings contain the inspiration that can help us discover the constantly emerging light that comes from Torah as it is refracted through its most passionate teachers.
Rabbi William H. Lebeau, Vice-Chancellor, Jewish Theological Seminary, New York

The vignettes leap off the page, not only aptly illustrating the truths Rabbi Elkins shares, but making those truths absolutely unforgettable. A keen observer of culture, he manages to gently educate - and even entertain, with rare skill. This volume will be invaluable to anyone open to the lively encounter of an historic tradition with the concerns of today.
Rabbi Stanley M. Davids, Atlanta

Rabbi Elkins displays in these chapters the immediacy and relevance of the modern preacher together with the breadth of learning of the great Darshanim of the past.
Rabbi David H. Lincoln, New York

A unique array of ideas, thoughts and insights that are lucid, concise, and to the point. In this age of sound-bytes, this book offers much to chew and to digest.
Rabbi Dr. Reuven P. Bulka, Ottawa, Ontario

ORDER FORM

GROWTH ASSOCIATES
HUMAN RELATIONS CONSULTANTS & PUBLISHERS
212 STUART RD. EAST, PRINCETON, NJ 08540
(609) 497-7375

PLEASE PRINT OR TYPE

NAME: _____ DATE: _____

ADDRESS: _____

CITY, STATE, ZIP: _____ TEL.: _____

EDUCATIONAL MATERIALS BY DR. DOV PERETZ ELKINS

Qty	Titles Available	Cost	Total
	Moments of Transcendence: Devotional Comments on the High Holiday Mahzor **Vol. I**: Rosh Hashanah, **Vol. II**: Yom Kippur. 1992 Supplement - 150 pages 1993 Supplement - 150 pages 2-Volume Hardcover edition (Jason Aronson, 1992) * NEW * 2 vols.	----- $20 $20 $60	
	Prescription For a Long & Happy Life - Age-Old Wisdom For the New Age * NEW * 1993- Hardcover - Sermons & Essays	$22	
	My Seventy-Two Friends: Encounters With Refuseniks in the USSR	$12	
	Organizational Development for Jewish Groups	$8	
	Experiential Programs for Jewish Groups: 30 full-length programs	$10	
	Clarifying Jewish Values: 25 Values Activities for Jewish Groups	$10	
	Jewish Consciousness Raising: 50 Experiential Exercises	$10	
	Loving My Jewishness: Jewish Self-Pride and Self-Esteem. A text for adult & teenage groups. Ten or more copies @ $5, including Leader's Guide.	$10	
	Teaching People to Love Themselves: A Leader's Handbook of Theory & Technique for Self-Esteem Training. Includes 50 experiential exercises. <u>Best seller</u>.	$22	
	Glad To Be Me: Building Self-Esteem in Yourself & Others Collection of readings & photos - Revised & Expanded Edition (1989)	$12	
	Twelve Pathways to Feeling Better About Yourself	$7.50	
	Self-Concept Source Book: Ideas & Activities for Building Self-Esteem	$19	
	The Ideal Jew: Values Clarification Program (Leader's guide + 15 cc.) set	$10	
	Why Did Susan Cohen Desert Judaism? Values Clarification set Program on Intermarriage, Assimilation, (Ldr's guide & 15 cc)	$10	
	God's Warriors: Dramatic Adventures of Rabbis in Uniform	$10	
	Rejoice With Jerusalem: Prayers, Readings, & Songs for Israel Observances	$6	
	The Tallit: Some Modern Meanings (Jewish Tract Series)	$3	

All orders must be prepaid.   Subtotal: _____

Postage & Handling: 15% of order; Canada & Foreign: 20% of order. (Minimum $3.)   Postage/handling: _____

Make checks payable to Dov Peretz Elkins (US Funds only).   **TOTAL ORDER:** _____

_____ Check here if interested in inviting Dr. Elkins to give lectures, workshops, retreats, and/or other training events for board, staff or faculty, etc.